how2become

JOIN THE ROYAL NAVY
The Insider's Guide

HODDER
EDUCATION
AN HACHETTE UK COMPANY

Orders: Please contact Bookpoint Ltd, 130 Milton Park, Abingdon, Oxon
OX14 4SB. Telephone: (44) 01235 827720, Fax: (44) 01235 400454. Lines
are open from 9.00 to 5.00, Monday to Saturday, with a 24-hour message
answering service.
You can also order through our website www.hoddereducation.co.uk

British Library Cataloguing in Publication Data
A catalogue record for this title is available from the British Library.

ISBN: 978 1444 110593

First published   2010
Impression number 10 9   8   7   6   5   4   3   2   1
Year   2015   2014   2013   2012   2011   2010

Typeset by Servis Filmsetting Ltd, Stockport, Cheshire
Printed in Great Britain for Hodder Education, An Hachette UK Company,
338 Euston Road, London NW1 3BH by Cox & Wyman Ltd, Reading,
Berkshire.

Hachette UK's policy is to use papers that are natural, renewable and
recyclable products and made from wood grown in sustainable forests.
The logging and manufacturing processes are expected to conform to the
environmental regulations of the country of origin.

JOIN THE ROYAL NAVY
The Insider's Guide

CONTENTS

THE ROYAL NAVY SELECTION INTERVIEW

INTRODUCTION

Welcome to how2become: *Join the Royal Navy: The Insider's Guide*. This guide has been designed to help you prepare for, and pass the Royal Navy selection process that is applicable for a Rating.

The author of this guide, Richard McMunn, spent more than 20 years in both the Royal Navy and the Fire and Rescue Service. He has vast experience and knowledge in the area of Armed Forces' recruitment and you will find his guidance both inspiring and informative. During his highly successful career in the Fire Service, Richard sat on many interview panels assessing candidates to join the service. He has also been extremely successful at passing job interviews himself and has a success rate of more than 90 per cent. Follow his advice and preparation techniques carefully and you too can achieve the same levels of success in your career. While the selection process for joining the Royal Navy is highly competitive there are a number of things you can do in order to improve your chances of success, and they are all contained within this book. The book has been divided into useful sections to make it easier for you to prepare for each

stage. Read each section carefully and take notes as you progress. Don't ever give up on your dreams; if you really want to join the Navy then you *can* do it. The way to prepare for a job in the Armed Forces is to embark on a programme of 'in-depth' preparation, and this book will show you exactly how to do that.

If you need any further help with the Royal Navy Recruiting Test, getting fit or Royal Navy interview advice, we offer a wide range of products to assist you. These are all available through our online shop www.how2become.co.uk. Once again thank you for your custom and we wish you every success in your pursuit of a career in the Royal Navy.

Work hard, stay focused and be what you want …

Best wishes

The how2become team

The how2become Team

PREFACE

by author Richard McMunn

I applied to join the Royal Navy when I was 16 years old. I lived in a town called Leyland in Lancashire with my parents and I attended Balshaw's Grammar School. I didn't do particularly well at school, which was purely down to my own individual lack of focus, but to me three GCSEs at grade C or above was just fine. Outside school I was running my own mobile car-washing business and I was making about £80 a weekend. I used to get up early every Saturday and Sunday morning and cycle round to my customers' houses with buckets of water and wash their cars while they were asleep. When they woke up their car was cleaned and I'd get my £3 for doing a good job! When I look back now I realise how hard I used to work, something which has stood me in good stead for the rest of my life. To me, educational qualifications are great, but they are no replacement for hard graft, common sense and they certainly don't guarantee to make a person a good employee. Now, I'm not saying that a person should intentionally do badly at school, because that is not true. If I had my time again I would work a lot harder at school, that's for sure. What I am saying is that you can still achieve lots

in life with little or no qualifications. Since I left school with my three GCSEs I have had a great career in the Royal Navy, winning an award for being one of the best recruits, a 16-year exemplary career in the Fire Service rising to the rank of Station Manager, been an HSBC award winning start up entrepreneur, and now a published author, all before my 38th birthday. Anything is possible.

I love helping people achieve what they want in life and through this book that is what I intend to do for you. So, before we get started I want you to put any negative thoughts out of your mind and I want you to read the book carefully. Once you have finished reading the book, I want you to work very hard at improving yourself so that you can successfully pass the Royal Navy selection process. I had a truly fantastic time in the Royal Navy and it is a career that I would recommend to anyone.

Success doesn't come easy

I can remember sitting in the Armed Forces Careers Office in Preston, Lancashire, at the age of 16 waiting patiently to see the Warrant Officer who would interview me as part of my application for joining the Royal Navy. I had already passed the written tests, and despite never having sat an interview before in my life, I was confident of success.

In the build-up to the interview I had worked very hard studying the job that I was applying for, and also working hard on my interview technique. At the end of the interview I was told that I had easily passed and all that was left to complete was the medical. Unfortunately, I was overweight at the time and I was worried that I might fail. At the medical my fears became a reality and I was told by the doctor that I would have to lose a stone (6 kg) in weight before they would accept me. I walked out of the doctor's surgery to the bus stop to catch the bus that would take me back home, three miles away. I was absolutely gutted, and embarrassed, that I had failed at the final hurdle, all because I was overweight!

I sat at the bus stop feeling sorry for myself and wondering what job I was going to apply for next. My dream of joining the Armed Forces was over and I didn't know which way to turn. Suddenly, I began to feel a sense of determination to lose the weight and get fit in the shortest time possible. It was at that point in my life when things changed forever. As the bus approached I remember thinking there was no time like the present for getting started on my fitness regime. I therefore opted to walk the three miles home instead of being lazy and getting the bus. When I got home I sat in my room and wrote out a 'plan of action' that would dictate how I was going to lose the weight required. That plan of action was very simple and it said the following three things:

1. Every weekday morning I will get up at 6a.m. and run three miles.

2. Instead of catching the bus to college and then back home again I will walk.

3. I will eat healthily and I will not go over the recommended daily calorific intake.

Every day I would read my simple 'action plan' and it acted as a reminder of what I needed to do. Within a few weeks of following my plan rigidly I had lost over a stone in weight and I was a lot fitter too!

When I returned to the doctor's surgery for my medical, the doctor was amazed that I had managed to lose the weight in such a short space of time and he was pleased that I had been so determined to pass the medical. Six months later I started my basic training course with the Royal Navy.

Ever since then I have always made sure that I prepare properly for any job application. If I do fail a particular interview or section of an application process then I will always go out of my way to ask for feedback so that I can improve for next time. I also still use an 'action plan' in just about every element of my work today. Action plans allow you to focus

your mind on what you want to achieve and in this guide I will be teaching you how to use them to great effect.

Throughout my career I have always been successful. It's not because I am better than the next person, but simply because I prepare effectively. I didn't do very well at school so I have to work a lot harder to pass the exams and written tests that form part of a job application process but I am always aware of what I need to do and what I must improve on.

I have always been a great believer in preparation. Preparation was my key to success, and it's also yours. Without the right level of preparation you will be setting out on the route to failure. The Royal Navy is hard to join, but if you follow the steps that I have compiled within this guide and use them as part of your preparation then you will increase your chances of success dramatically.

The men and women of the Armed Forces carry out an amazing job. They are there to protect us and our country, and they do that job with great pride, passion and very high levels of professionalism and commitment. They are to be congratulated for the job that they do. Before you apply to join the Navy you need to be fully confident that you, too, are capable of providing that same level of commitment. If you think you can do it, and you can rise to the challenge, then you just might be the type of person the Royal Navy is looking for.

CHAPTER I
WHAT'S IT LIKE IN THE ROYAL NAVY?

I can only speak from my personal experience and that of other people whom I've spoken to during the research into this book, but the simple answer is that it's a fantastic career! It's certainly not an easy career in respect of being away from home for many weeks and even months at a time, but it is still an amazing career nonetheless. I joined the Royal Navy as an Aircraft Engineer in the Fleet Air Arm and I served with 800 Naval Air Squadron on HMS *Invincible* during the early 1990s. I met lots of brilliant and talented people during my career and I formed a number of very close friendships along the way. I'd also been around the world by the time I was 19 and visited places that others only ever dream about.

I can remember boarding the train at Preston station on 13 April 1989 that would take me to HMS *Raleigh* for my initial training course. I'd been away from home before for a couple of weeks at the most during a school Geography field trip and a Scout trip, but nothing could prepare me for the basic training course that I was about to be put through. My parents and my girlfriend at the

time waved me off from the platform. As the train departed I sat there with a combined feeling of adventure and apprehension. The train journey from Preston to HMS *Raleigh* was a long one, about seven hours I seem to recall, just enough time for me to get even more nervous before the recruit training course started. Even though it was many years ago I can still picture the Leading Hand who met me at Torpoint train station. As the train pulled in he stood there with his clipboard and stick. Just the look of him was enough to make me want to turn around and go back home! I was amazed at how many people I'd been sitting with on the same train who were also on the Phase One training course. None of us had even realised or spoken to each other during the entire train journey. We all stood there on the platform with our bags and suitcases waiting to be told what to do by the fearsome looking Leading Hand. He carried out a roll call and once he was satisfied that everyone was in attendance we all boarded the blue Sherpa van and headed off to HMS *Raleigh* where we would start our basic training.

Over the next few weeks I learnt how to iron (properly), clean my shoes (properly), got fit and learnt everything about the Royal Navy you could possibly cram into six weeks. It was an intense initiation into the service but it felt great to be a part of such an organisation. You see, when you join an organisation like this everyone looks out for each other and you also get to forge very close friendships along the way. During my career in the Navy I met loads of brilliant people. Some of the more memorable friendships were with Andy Salter, Steve Doubleday (I think he's a pilot now), Mike Tolley, Steve 'Smudge' Smith, Darryl 'Bomber' Brown, Stu Brown, Tiny O'Grady and Steve Lomas, all great people with whom I shared some unbelievable times.

Once I'd completed my basic training course I then spent the next ten months or so at HMS *Daedalus* in Gosport. Here I learnt how to become an Aircraft Engineer working with weapons, ejector seats and also on the electrical systems of an aircraft. It was a steep learning curve but I loved every minute of it. Once my trade training was complete, I went off to serve with 899 Harrier Squadron which was based at

Royal Naval Air Station (RNAS) Yeovilton at the time. I would basically 'cut my teeth' with 899 Squadron and learn how to service and repair Harrier jets under close supervision before finally being let loose on my own with 800 Squadron. Although based at RNAS Yeovilton, 800 Sqaudron was assigned to HMS *Invincible*. My first ever trip with HMS *Invincible* was only a few weeks long, during sea trials just off the coast of Norway. If you've ever seen an aircraft carrier such as the *Invincible* you will know that it has a 'ski ramp'. The ski ramp is basically a steep incline from which the fixed-wing aircraft take off. If you are part of a Harrier Squadron upon an aircraft carrier then you get the unfortunate experience of sleeping directly below the ski ramp! During my time on *Invincible*, Harriers would take off, usually six at a time, at all times of the day. If you were trying to sleep directly below the ramp at the time of take off then you were usually unsuccessful, as you can imagine. Shifts onboard ship for me usually consisted of eight hours on, eight hours off continuous without many rest days. This shift system was applicable to my squadron only and the other members of the ship's company would work different hours. All I can remember is that every member of the ship's company would work his or her socks off throughout the duration of the trip, even if the trip was for months at a time. It's true what they say; while we all sleep comfortably at night in our homes thousands of British Armed Forces men and women are working tirelessly to protect us and our country. For all the hard work, however, there would be the odd 'run ashore'. A run ashore is basically a trip off the boat to dry land where you can go and let your hair down, sample the local culture and have a few sociable drinks. I had some great runs ashore in places such as Barbados, Portugal, America, Italy, Africa, Spain and Greece. Of course, you have to be on your best behaviour at all times as the last thing you want is to get into trouble while in another country. However, follow the rules, don't do anything stupid and you can have a great time in the process.

After serving a few years in the Navy I decided that it was time to follow my lifetime ambition of becoming a firefighter.

I could have quite easily stayed in the Navy for 22 years but I had always set my heart on fighting fires. I was very young when I joined the Navy but I believe the experiences that I gained during my service set me up for a bright and successful future in the Fire Service. The Royal Navy taught me how to be disciplined, it taught me how to get organised and it also taught me how to look after myself. When I joined the Fire Service following my career in the Navy I literally breezed through the selection process and I passed the initial firefighter training course with relative ease. This was simply due to the fact that I was self-disciplined and I knew how to prepare effectively, all as a result of my experiences in the Navy. One thing the Navy didn't prepare me for, however, was sea sickness. I spent months aboard HMS *Invincible* during some of the most treacherous sea conditions imaginable and I was never sea sick. However, after I passed my initial firefighter training course I was assigned to White Watch at Maidstone Fire Station. During the first few weeks on the watch I was invited to go on a sea fishing trip in a small boat just off the coast of Dover. I've never been so sea sick in all my life. How embarrassing!

The Navy is one of the few jobs where an employer, in this case the Government, is willing to take you on without any previous work experience or qualifications. Show them that you're worth the investment during the selection process, and they will develop you into a competent and professional person during your career. When I left the Navy to join the Fire Service I was a totally different man from when I first joined. At the age of 21 I had been around the world, I was physically fit, and I had a number of extremely useful qualifications under my belt. I will always be grateful to the Royal Navy for giving me the opportunity that they did.

So, now it's your turn. But before you join you will need to work hard in order to pass the selection process. In order to help you prepare effectively for the selection process I have divided this book into 'easy to use' sections. Read the book carefully and take notes as you progress.

CHAPTER 2
THE ROYAL NAVY SELECTION PROCESS FOR RATINGS

Before we get into the main elements of the book let's take a quick look at what the selection process for joining the Navy as a Rating actually involves.

The selection process is divided into different sections, all designed to assess your suitability for joining. The selection process isn't just a test for test's sake; it's a carefully prepared process that will give the Royal Navy a very good indication as to what you will perform like as an employee. As I indicated at the start of this book you do not need any qualifications for many of the jobs the Royal Navy has to offer, but you still need to pass the selection process. Just because a person has lots of qualifications doesn't guarantee that they will be an exceptional employee.

Step 1 – Make contact with your Armed Forces Careers Office

The first step on your route to joining the Royal Navy as a Rating is to make contact with your local Armed Forces careers adviser. Joining the Royal Navy is a very big decision and one that shouldn't be taken lightly. You will need to consider your choice of career carefully and who better to discuss this with than you local Armed Forces careers adviser. He or she will be able to provide you with details and information about the Royal Navy and the career options that are available to you, including a presentation and recruitment literature. You will also be required to complete a short questionnaire that will determine your suitability for joining.

The Royal Navy has many different career options available ranging from Aircraft Engineering Technician through to Chef and Medical Assistant. It is vital that you choose your career carefully and that you have valid reasons for your choice. When I joined I was totally set on wanting to be part of the Fleet Air Arm. A few years earlier I had visited a naval air base museum and was fascinated by the history of the Fleet Air Arm. In particular, I had a keen interest in Sea Harrier jets and I used to make model aircraft when I was younger. I admit, my hobby as a teenager didn't guarantee that I would make a good Sea Harrier engineer, but I could certainly prove that I had a passion for this kind of work during my Royal Navy interview. I was also a practical person through and through, and loved to see how things worked – even if this meant infuriating my parents by taking apart the portable radio and not being able to put it back together again!

You should also discuss your choice of career with your parents/guardian and your partner (if applicable). It is important that they support you in your decision and if they have any worries or concerns, which are only natural of course, then you may wish to take them along to the careers office with you. The first time I visited the careers office my father came along with me just to see what it was all about. He wanted to be sure, as any parent would, that his son wasn't joining a

tin-pot outfit. After five minutes of speaking with the Warrant Officer he was convinced that I was applying to join a very professional organisation. He was probably more relieved at the thought of his son leaving home to be totally honest!

So, your first step after reading this guide is to make contact with your local Armed Forces Careers Office. You can find the location of all AFCOs via the website www.royalnavy.mod.uk or you can call them on 08456 07 55 55 to find out more.

Tips for when making contact with your Armed Forces Careers Office

- Before you attend the interview you will need to get together your birth certificate, National Insurance number, NHS card, passport and educational certificates. If you do not have any of these documents then contact the AFCO to let them know before your interview.

- In the build-up to the initial interview you should read your recruitment literature thoroughly and also visit the Royal Navy website at www.royalnavy.mod.uk.

- Always be polite and demonstrate good manners when speaking to the AFCO careers adviser. First impressions are important and you will want to come across in a positive manner. This will work in your favour.

- Although it is not essential, I would advise that you attend the careers office dressed smartly. Now I am not saying you need to go out and buy an expensive suit, but I would recommend you are, clean and tidy. The majority of people who attend the careers office will go along in jeans and trainers. Remember that you are applying to join a uniformed, disciplined service. Just because you aren't a member of the Royal Navy yet doesn't mean to say you can't start acting like one.

- Before you make contact with the AFCO check the eligibility requirements for joining to see if you meet them. You can find the eligibility requirements on the website www.royalnavy.mod.uk.

Step 2 – Initial Armed Forces Careers Office interview

Once you have made contact with the AFCO, completed a questionnaire, watched a presentation and received your recruitment literature, you will need to attend your first interview. The first interview is more of an informal chat which is designed to assess the reasons why you want to join the Royal Navy and also to look at the skills, experiences and qualifications that you possess. The recruitment adviser will then be able to advise you on the type(s) of career that you may be more suited to. The first interview is a relatively informal affair and should last no longer than 30 minutes. The interview will normally be carried out by a Royal Navy careers adviser.

Step 3 – Sit the Royal Navy Recruiting Test

The Royal Navy Recruiting Test is basically a series of psychometric tests that are designed to assess your ability to meet the demands of the Royal Navy and your chosen career. The tests are a tried-and-tested method of selection and are extremely accurate in assessing a candidate's suitability. The pass mark required for each role will vary depending on the requirements for each job. The test itself will normally be carried out at your local Armed Forces Careers Office and will be under strict timed conditions. Once you have completed the test your Armed Forces careers adviser will discuss your results with you. This will normally be on the same day as the test.

Later in this book I have provided lots of sample test questions to help you prepare for the Recruiting Test.

The four different testing areas are as follows:

- A **reasoning test** – used to assess your ability to 'reason' and 'interpret' information that is placed in front of you. This will be in the format of written words, numbers or diagrams. In the actual test you will have 9 minutes in which to tackle the 30 questions.

- A **verbal ability test** – designed to assess your ability to understand words and the connection between those words. During this test you will again have 9 minutes in which to tackle the 30 questions.

- A **numerical reasoning test** – designed to assess how competent you are while working with basic numerical calculations such as addition, subtraction, multiplication, division, fractions, percentages and algebra. You will have 16 minutes to answer 30 questions during the actual test.

- A **mechanical comprehension test** – assesses your ability to understand mechanical concepts because many jobs within the Royal Navy are practical, and therefore require an ability to understand mechanical concepts. During the real test you will have 10 minutes to complete the 30 questions.

Tips for preparing for the Royal Navy Recruiting Test

- In the build-up to the test practise lots of psychometric tests that are relevant to the real tests. In addition to practising the tests that are contained within this book I recommend you also obtain a psychometric testing book from www.how2become.co.uk. The more tests you do, the better.

- Practise little and often. In the next chapter I will show you how to create an 'action plan' for success. As part of this action plan you should dedicate plenty of time to the Royal Navy Recruiting Test over a prolonged period, as opposed to cramming the night before your test.

- Practise without the aid of a calculator and also practise under timed conditions. Put yourself under pressure in the build-up to the tests and you will find that the real tests seem far easier.

- At the end of each practice test you should check carefully to see which questions you got wrong. Then, learn from your errors. This is a crucial part of your development.

Step 4 – Royal Navy selection interview

Once you have successfully completed the Recruiting Test you will then be invited back for a selection interview. The selection interview is far more in-depth than the first interview and you will need to carry out plenty of preparation. During the selection interview you will be asked questions that relate to the following areas:

- Personal details that relate to where you were born, the schools you attended, where you live and details about your family. They will also want to know whether you have a partner and what they think about you joining.

- Educational details including qualifications obtained and what you thought about your results. How many schools you attended and whether or not you travelled with your school. They will also want to assess your attitude towards education and what you think about your teachers.

- The reasons why you want to join the Royal Navy.

- The reasons why you have chosen the Royal Navy over the other services such as the Army or Royal Air Force.

- The qualities you have that will be of benefit to the service.

- What your parents/guardian think about you joining.

- Your hobbies and interests and also your sporting activities.

- Whether you are a member of any groups or youth organisations.

- What fitness activities you currently participate in.

- Your experiences of working as part of a team.

- Your experiences of being away from home and/or communal living (living with large groups of people).

- Responsibilities that you have either at home, school or at work.

- How you feel you will cope with military life and being away from home.

- What you already know about the Royal Navy, its lifestyle, history and the training you will undergo while at HMS *Raleigh*.

- Why you have chosen your particular career and what you know about the role and the training you will undergo.

In a separate section of this guide I have provided you with in-depth information on how to prepare for the selection interview.

Tips for passing the Royal Navy selection interview

- Prepare responses to the sample interview questions that I have provided within this book.

- Before you attend the actual selection interview I recommend you try out a number of mock interviews. This involves getting your parents or a friend to ask you the interview questions that are contained within this book. Try responding to the interview questions and see how you get on. When you attend the real interview you will have more confidence.

- Don't be late for your interview and make an effort to dress smartly. Try as hard as you can to make a positive impression. Never slouch in the interview chair and maintain eye contact with the interviewer.

Step 5 – Medical and eye test

Once you have passed the selection interview you will be required to pass a medical and an eye test. Your recruitment adviser will provide you with further details relating to each of these tests.

Step 6 – The Royal Navy Pre-Joining Fitness Test (PJFT)

During the selection process you will be required to pass the Royal Navy Pre-Joining Fitness test which consists of a 1.5-mile run. The test is usually carried out at a local gym or fitness centre on a treadmill. At the time of writing the standard for the PJFT is as follows:

Age	Men	Women
15 to 24	12 minutes 20 seconds	14 minutes 35 seconds
25 to 29	12 minutes 48 seconds	15 minutes 13 seconds
30 to 34	13 minutes 18 seconds	15 minutes 55 seconds
35 to 39	13 minutes 49 seconds	16 minutes 40 seconds

The test itself is designed to assess your ability to pass the Phase One Royal Navy training course. If you can reach the required standard then there is a good chance that you will pass the fitness tests that form part of initial training. In a later section I have provided a free 'How to Get Navy Fit' guide which will assist you during your preparation for the PJFT.

Step 7 – Final interviews and tests (if applicable), and security/reference checks

The final stages of selection may include further specialist interviews and tests, but these are applicable only to certain jobs/trades. Your AFCO adviser will provide you with details of these if they relate to your specific career choice. It is at this stage that the Royal Navy will make certain security and reference checks. When you provide the names of people who will give references at the start of your application bear in mind the following points:

- One of your referees will be either your head teacher or your current/previous employer. It is important to approach them first to check that they are happy for you to nominate them as a referee.

- Whoever else you choose as a referee be sure that they are going to provide you with an honest and suitable reference. You do not want to get this far along the selection process and fail owing to a poor reference.

- Ask your nominated referees to provide you with a copy of what they have written about you. If you are asked any questions relative to the references provided then you can be prepared with a suitable response.

Once you have completed and successfully passed every stage of the selection process you will be offered a starting date for your basic training which will take place at HMS *Raleigh*.

CHAPTER 3
HOW TO CREATE AN ACTION PLAN FOR SUCCESS

In this early chapter of the book I want to explain a little bit about how I use 'action plans' to great effect in the majority of work/career related things that I do. I also want you to use an action plan when preparing for the Royal Navy selection process so it is important that you understand how they work.

In order to explain what an action plan is I will use a simple day-to-day task that many of us carry out. Let us assume that you or your parents are going to go on a large weekly food shop. Before you go shopping you or your parents will take a look in the fridge and the cupboards to see what's missing. You will then write down a list of what you need to buy while on your shopping trip. You will refer to your list to make sure that you buy the goods that you need in order to get through the forthcoming week. This is a simple yet highly effective process. Let's now apply the same principle to our Royal Navy selection process preparation.

After reading this book you realise that you have quite a lot of preparation to put into your application. So, to begin with, let's write down each area that you may need to improve on:

Improvement area 1
My knowledge of the Royal Navy, its history, the basic training and lifestyle.

Improvement area 2
My knowledge of my chosen career and the training that I will undergo.

Improvement area 3
My ability to pass the Royal Navy Recruiting Test and in particular the four psychometric testing elements.

Improvement area 4
My fitness levels so that I can pass the Pre-Joining Fitness Test with ease.

Improvement area 5
My interview technique and my responses to the anticipated interview questions.

Once we've detailed each area that we need to work on we can then create an action plan that will ensure we improve on those areas. Here's an example of what a weekly action plan might consist of:

Sample action plan

The action plan (opposite) is only an example of how it might look. Your action plan may be totally different as you will probably have different time constraints due to work, education or family commitments. However, I still believe it is very important to use a structured action plan while preparing for selection. It is also very important that you print out your action plan and stick it in a prominent position somewhere such as on the fridge or on your bedroom wall. Each day that you achieve something, tick it off as complete, and you will start to feel good about yourself and the progress that

Monday	Tuesday	Wednes-day	Thurs-day	Friday	Satur-day	Sunday
30 minutes psycho-metric test prepar-ation and 30 minutes reading up on Royal Navy life, history and training	60 minutes study relating to my choice of career and the training I will undergo	60 minutes psycho-metric test prepar-ation	Rest day	30 minutes psycho-metric test prepar-ation and 30 minutes reading up on Royal Navy life, history and training	60 minutes study relating to my choice of career and the training I will undergo	60 minutes psycho-metric test prepar-ation and 30 minutes reading up on Royal Navy life, history and training
1.5-mile run at my best effort (record time)	45 minutes gym work (light weights)	1.5-mile run followed by 30 minutes interview prepar-ation		1.5-mile run (best effort) and interview prepar-ation	45 minutes gym work (light weights) or 30-minute swim	3-mile run (best effort) and interview prepar-ation

you are making. Using an action plan is also a great way to demonstrate to the interviewer that you have implemented some form of structure or routine to your life. Take a look at the following sample interview question and response.

Sample interview question

When you join the Royal Navy you will need to follow a set routine each day. To some, this will come as a shock. Tell me about a time when you've implemented some form of structure or routine into your life.

Sample response

In the build-up to selection I have been working very hard at improving myself in a number of different areas. In order to achieve this I implemented a structured action plan that set out what I was going to do and more importantly when I was going to do it. For example, each morning I would get up at 6a.m. and go running 1.5 miles in preparation for the early starts that I will have during my career, and also so that I can comfortably pass the PJFT. Before I went to work I would sit down for 30 minutes and work on my psychometric testing so that I could pass the Recruiting Test. Once I got home from work I would sit down for 60 minutes and study the Royal Navy, its history, lifestyle and my choice of career. I have found that by implementing an action plan into my daily routine I improved a lot quicker in these important areas. I fully understand that routine and structure are important parts of Navy life so I have been preparing for this in the build-up to selection.

Your action plan for success

During your preparation implement an action plan that dictates the areas in which you need to improve. On the next page I have provided an action plan template for you to use.

Tips for creating an effective action plan

- Before you create your action plan write down the key areas that you need to improve on.

- Within your action plan include times, dates and the length of time that you intend to work on each area.

- Include at least one rest day each week of your action plan.

- Vary your action plan on a weekly basis to maintain concentration levels and interest.

My action plan for success

Monday	Tuesday	Wednesday	Thursday	Friday	Saturday	Sunday

CHAPTER 4
THE ASSESSABLE QUALITIES AND HOW TO MATCH THEM

In this chapter I will provide information that relates to how the Royal Navy will assess you during the selection process. The criteria that I am going to give you relate to your own personal attributes, qualities and also your knowledge of the Royal Navy and your chosen career. This information will act as a good foundation for your preparation. If you are capable of providing the Royal Navy selecting officers with what they are looking for then your chances of success will greatly increase.

The assessable qualities

The following list is an example of some of the criteria used during the selection process:

- Personal turnout and hygiene
- Physical fitness

- Sociability
- Emotional maturity and stability
- Drive and determination to succeed
- Experience of being self-reliant
- Reactions to discipline
- Experience of and reaction to regimentation and routine
- Knowledge and experience of Royal Navy life
- Motivation to join the Royal Navy
- Personal circumstances.

This list is not exhaustive and there will be other areas on which the Royal Navy will be assessing you during the interviews and the written tests. However, having an understanding of the qualities you need to demonstrate throughout selection will improve your chances of success dramatically.

In order to provide you with a greater understanding of what is required I will now go into more detail about each specific area.

Personal turnout and hygiene

Picture the scene; you have joined the Royal Navy and you are sharing sleeping quarters with 30 other people onboard ship. One of your work colleagues, who sleeps near to you, has very poor personal hygiene. How do you think you'd feel? Apart from the risk of germs spreading it isn't particularly nice living in a bunk next to someone who doesn't wash often. Believe me I know!

When you attend the careers office make an effort in both your personal turnout and your personal hygiene. Don't go there straight from the building site. The recruitment staff will want to see that you have made an effort to present yourself positively. When you attend the careers office, whether it is for

an interview or a careers presentation, always make sure you wear a formal outfit such as a suit. While this is not essential it will allow you to score higher in this important area.

Many people will stroll into the careers office wearing jeans and trainers. Make an effort to stand out for the right reasons and this will certainly work in your favour. Those people who turn up to the Armed Forces Careers Office dressed untidily and unwashed will score poorly. Throughout this book I will make reference to the importance of dressing smartly and making the effort to present yourself in a positive, motivated and professional manner.

> ### Tips for scoring high marks in personal turnout and hygiene
>
> - Make sure your shoes are clean and polished.
> - Shirt, trousers and tie are ideal for males, and a smart formal outfit for females.
> - Ensure your clothes are ironed and not creased.
> - Work on your personal hygiene and overall appearance. Make sure your nails are clean!
> - Stand tall and be confident.
> - Don't slouch in the interview chair.

Physical fitness

There are two elements here that need to be addressed. With the advent of the computer and electronic games more people, especially younger people, are spending longer hours at the computer. The average person now spends approximately 25 minutes every day using the computer and that figure is set to rise as the years progress. We are less active now as a nation than we have ever been, which leads to only one thing – a decrease in physical fitness levels. When you join the Royal Navy you will be joining an organisation that requires its men

and women to be both physically active and physically fit. Therefore, the recruitment staff will want to see evidence of these two important attributes during selection. They are very easy to demonstrate. If you do little or no physical exercise at present then now is the time to change. At the end of this book I have provided a fitness guide that contains a number of useful exercises, the majority of which can be carried out without the need to attend a gym. Embark on a structured training programme in the build-up to selection and you will score higher in this area.

Tips for scoring high marks in physical fitness

- Implement a structured training programme within your action plan.

- Play team sports or take up some form of outdoor activity.

- Consider joining the Sea Cadets or some other form of youth organisation.

Sociability

This quality assesses your ability to mix well with people. What are you like with groups of people? Can you mix well and have you ever slept in a room with lots of other people before? When I started my basic training at HMS *Raleigh* it was a strange experience sharing a room with about 30 other people. On the first night we were all sitting in the corridor trying hard to 'bull' our boots. Nobody had a clue what to do but we all stayed there until we got it right. You have to be able to mix with people from all walks of life and all ages in the Royal Navy, and if you aren't much of a sociable person now then you certainly will be by the end of your training! During your basic training course you will find that everybody is there to help each other out and by the time your passing out parade arrives you'll be a totally different person. Those

applicants who come across as quiet or shy will not score well in the area of sociability. At no point during selection process should you be brash, abrasive or not a team player.

Tips for scoring high marks in sociability

- During the interviews provide examples of when you have mixed well with others. This may be through youth organisations such as the Sea Cadets or Scouts.

- If you have played team sports then this will be an advantage.

- Tell the interviewer that you will have no problem with communal living. Communal living is living with other people. You may be in a room of up to 30 other people while in your training, so the interviewer will want to know that you are comfortable with this.

- Smile and laugh where appropriate – a sense of humour is a must, but you should never be overbearing or overconfident. Never 'back chat' or be disrespectful to the recruitment staff.

Emotional maturity and stability

The Royal Navy wants to see that you are mature for your age and that you are even tempered and well balanced. It doesn't want people who are aggressive or who come across with a bad attitude. The interviewer wants to see that you have coped well with the ups and downs of life so far and you may find that they ask you questions on any difficult areas of life that you have had to deal with. They want to know that you will adapt well to the change in lifestyle when you join the Royal Navy and that you can cope in highly stressful situations. They will also be looking for you to be mature for your age and that there are no signs of depression or anxiety. They will also be assessing your ability to cope well with unfamiliar surroundings and that you will not become homesick during training.

Tips for scoring high marks in emotional maturity and stability

- During the interviews and during discussions with the Armed Forces Careers Office adviser try to provide examples of when you have dealt well with difficult situations in your life in a positive and mature manner.

- Try to be upbeat and positive about the future.

- Don't be overconfident or macho.

Drive and determination to succeed

Would you say that you're a driven person who is determined to succeed? Well, you've got this far through the book so the answer is probably yes!

The Royal Navy wants to know that you have a sense of purpose in your life. The interviewer will be looking for a pattern of achievement, either through school or at work, and for evidence that you are not easily deflected from your goals and aspirations. You will recall at the beginning of this book how much emphasis I put on perseverance. Drive and determination are similar to perseverance in that you have the ability to keep working hard and improving yourself until you achieve success. Those applicants who show signs that they give up easily or have no goals or aspirations will score poorly in this area.

Tips for scoring high marks in drive and determination to succeed

- Provide examples of when you have achieved a goal. This might be educational qualifications, courses that you have attended or even sporting achievements.

- Be positive about joining the Royal Navy and tell the interviewer that nothing is going to stop you from

succeeding. If you don't pass this time then you will look for ways to improve for the next time you apply.

- Demonstrate that your ambition and sense of purpose is to join the Royal Navy and become a professional and competent Rating.

Experience of being self-reliant

During your Royal Navy career you will need to be self-reliant, especially because you'll be spending many months away from home at any given time. If you can't look after yourself now then there's little chance that you'll be able to look after yourself during training and also on board ship. During the selection process you should provide the recruitment staff with examples of when you have been away from home for lengthy periods or where you have had to cope on your own. Basically they want to know that you can look after yourself without the help of your parents or home comforts.

If you have no experience whatsoever of being self-reliant then I advise that you take steps to improve your experience in this area. For example, there is nothing to stop you from going camping for the weekend or joining the Sea Cadets where you will be able to gain experience of this important attribute.

Tips for scoring high marks in experience of being self-reliant

- Provide examples of when you have been away from home for short or long periods of time.

- Tell the interviewer that you enjoy travelling and being away from home. Remember that it is important to provide examples of when you have already done this.

(Continued)

 **how2become**

(Continued)

- Tell the interviewer that you are looking forward to leaving home to join the Royal Navy and facing the challenges that it presents.

- Provide examples of when you have had to fend for yourself or when you have been away camping.

Reactions to discipline

I can remember during my Royal Navy interview being asked a strange question by the Warrant Officer. He said to me 'What do you think about your teachers? Do they do a good job?' Fortunately, I had respect for people in positions of authority so the answer I gave was the correct one. My father was quite disciplined with me during my upbringing so respect for others came naturally. However, I am aware of a friend who failed to get in the Army because he gave a negative response to this type of question. He basically responded by saying that he felt his teacher was a bit of an idiot and that all the pupils could easily wind him up. That was the end of his chances! As soon as he said it he knew it was the wrong thing to say.

The Royal Navy wants to see that you have a positive attitude towards authority. People in authority include the police, your parents, teachers and even your boss at work. When you join the Royal Navy you will be taking orders from senior officers and the Navy wants to know that you have no problem with authority. There is a strong possibility that the interviewer will ask you questions that relate to your attitude to education and your teachers. At no point should you be negative about your teachers or about people who are in positions of authority. If you are disrespectful or negative about these people then there is a strong possibility that the Royal Navy selection officers will take a dim view of your attitude.

Tips for scoring high marks in reactions to discipline

- Provide examples of when you have carried out orders, either at work or at school.

- Tell the interviewer that you respect authority, providing you do of course, and that you see it as an important aspect of life. You do not have a problem with taking orders from anyone, even if they are of the opposite sex to you.

Experience of and reaction to regimentation and routine

When you join the Royal Navy you will lose much of your personal freedom. During your initial training there will be many restrictions placed upon you in terms of leave and your general freedom. This was one of the areas I found quite difficult when I first joined. Although I was young I was used to leading an active life, going out with my friends most evenings and playing football. As soon as I joined the Royal Navy I lost that personal freedom for a while. During the evenings there's plenty of study and preparation to do for the following day. You won't be given the time to do all of the things that you usually do while at home. Therefore, the Royal Navy wants to see that you have the ability to cope with this added pressure and the disciplined routine.

You must demonstrate during the selection process that you have already experienced some form of routine and that you are capable of following rules and regulations. This could simply be by having some form of disciplined routine at home, whereby you are required to clean the house and carry out the ironing for a few hours every week.

Tips for scoring high marks in experience of and reaction to regimentation and routine

- Provide examples of when you have lost your personal freedom, either during your upbringing, at school or

(Continued)

 how2become

(Continued)

> during work. Maybe you have had to work unsociable hours or had to dedicate time and effort to your educational studies?
>
> - Tell the interviewer that you fully understand that you will lose your personal freedom when you join the Royal Navy and that it won't be a problem for you.
>
> - Implement some form of routine into your preparation strategy for joining the Navy. Set out your action plan early on and follow it rigidly.

Knowledge and experience of Royal Navy life

During your preparation for joining the Royal Navy you will need to carry out plenty of research. This can be achieved simply by visiting the Royal Navy's website at www.royalnavy.mod.uk and also by reading your recruitment literature. Make sure you structure into your action plan plenty of time for this form of study.

In addition to studying the Royal Navy you may also wish to consider visiting a Navy establishment or museum. You should also ask questions of the recruitment staff to see what it's like to serve in the modern-day Navy. They will be able to provide you with an invaluable insight.

> ### Tips for scoring high marks in knowledge and experience of Royal Navy life
>
> - Speak to any friends or relatives who are members of the Armed Forces and ask them what it is like. Gain as much information as possible from the Armed Forces Careers Office staff and also through your recruitment literature.
>
> - Find out as much as possible about the training you will undertake when you join the Royal Navy for your chosen

career and also your initial training. This can be done by visiting the Navy's website.

- Consider visiting a Royal Navy establishment or museum. These are great places to learn about Navy life. You will need to book an appointment prior to your visit.

- Consider joining a youth organisation such as the Sea Cadets or Scouts to gain some experience of a disciplined service.

Motivation to join the Royal Navy

How motivated are you to join the Royal Navy? Do you want to join, or do you *really* want to join? The decision to join should be solely yours and not your parents' or guardians'. The Royal Navy will want to see that you have thought about this choice in career carefully and that you are fully confident in your decision. During the interview you will be asked two simple questions:

1. Why do you want to join the Royal Navy?

2. Why have you chosen the Royal Navy and not the other forces?

You should think about your responses to these questions carefully. The obvious major difference between the Royal Navy and the other forces is that you will be required to serve on board a ship. Weeks can go by before you see land again and if you choose to join as a submariner then it can be weeks before you even see daylight!

Tips for scoring high marks in motivation to join the Royal Navy

- Always present a positive attitude towards joining when you visit the Armed Forces Careers Office. This choice of career should be something that you have considered

---

(Continued)

(Continued)

> very carefully, and you have been working very hard to make sure that you pass.
>
> • Think about what attracts you to the Royal Navy and tell the interviewer during selection.

Personal circumstances

The Royal Navy wants to know that you have the support of your family and/or your partner. The interviewer also wants to see that you are free from any detracting circumstances such as financial difficulties. If you are in financial difficulty then this could have a negative effect on your mental health during training. They will assess your personal circumstances during the selection interview.

Tips for scoring high marks in personal circumstances

• Speak to your parents/guardian and your partner (if applicable) about your choice of career. Ask them for their support.

• Show your parents the Royal Navy website. There is a specific section on the site for parents and guardians.

• If they do not support you or they are concerned about you joining then I would recommend that you take them along to the careers office so that the Armed Forces careers officer can talk to them about Navy life and answer any questions that they may have. It is imperative that you have their full support.

How effective are you in each of the assessable qualities?

In order to measure how currently effective you are in each of the assessable qualities, look at the table on the following page and place a circle around the number which you believe reflects you best in each of the different areas. For example, scoring yourself as a 5 in 'knowledge of the Royal Navy' means that you are fully confident you could answer questions competently in this subject area. A score of 1 means you have plenty of work to do in this area. Finally, in the 'notes' box on the right-hand side of each assessable area, write what action you intend to take in order to improve.

Once you've completed the table you will have an action plan and a good idea of what you need to do in order to improve in each area.

Table of assessable qualities – an action plan for improvement

Assessable quality	Score					Notes
Personal turnout and hygiene	1	2	3	4	5	
Physical fitness	1	2	3	4	5	
Sociability	1	2	3	4	5	
Emotional maturity and stability	1	2	3	4	5	
Drive and determination to succeed	1	2	3	4	5	
Experience of being self-reliant	1	2	3	4	5	
Reactions to discipline	1	2	3	4	5	
Experience of and reaction to regimentation and routine	1	2	3	4	5	
Knowledge and experience of Royal Navy life	1	2	3	4	5	
Motivation to join the Royal Navy	1	2	3	4	5	
Personal circumstances	1	2	3	4	5	

CHAPTER 5
THE TOP TEN INSIDER TIPS AND ADVICE FOR SUCCESS

In this chapter I have provided you with my top ten tips and advice for success. While many of them will appear to be obvious I strongly recommend that you implement them into your preparation strategy.

1 Plan for success and look continually for ways to improve

As I have already stated, I am a big fan of preparation and I urge you to be the same. Too many people nowadays are not prepared to work hard in order to achieve their goals; they want things handed to them on a plate. Unfortunately, life isn't like that and if you really want something then you have to be prepared to put the effort in. If you work hard in the build-up to selection then you will reap the rewards and you will earn yourself a fantastic career. The Royal Navy will be very good to you as an employer and it will not only take

you around the world but it will pay you for the privilege. How many jobs can you say that about? Not many, that's for sure. The way to plan for success is to use an action plan and force yourself to work hard each and every day while you are going through selection. Write down the areas in which you need to improve and take positive action in order to ensure the improvements are made.

2 Use an action plan and set realistic targets

As stated in the previous chapter you should use an action plan in order to achieve success. Trust me, it works. Get used to writing down your goals and you will achieve them far easier and faster than if you don't use one. Your action plan must include the specific areas in which you want to improve. Depending on the level of improvement you want to make you may need to break down your goals into smaller stepping stones. For example, if you feel that you are overweight or unfit and you cannot run half a mile let alone 1.5 miles then you should break down your goal into manageable portions. During week one aim to walk 20 minutes a day, for four days at a brisk pace. Then, during the second week increase the walk to 30 minutes a day for five days. During the third week try running for half a mile and then walking 30 minutes for five days a week. Before you know it you'll be jogging and eventually you'll be able to reach the 1.5-mile run in the required time. As part of your action plan you should also set yourself a deadline for achieving your goal. Let's assume that your Royal Navy Recruiting Test is four weeks away. Design your action plan so that by the end of the third week you are fully conversant in the use of each of the four testing areas. This will leave you the fourth week to make any final tweaks and adjustments before sitting the real test.

Finally, as with any achievement you make in life you should celebrate your success. Once you have reached each milestone or achieved your goal of joining the Royal Navy then you should celebrate. I can remember when I finally passed my Royal Navy medical we all went out to celebrate with a family meal.

By celebrating your success you will be making achievement contagious and you will want to do it time and time again!

3 Choose the right career

During the initial stages of the selection process you will be asked to select a number of career options in your order of priority. Make sure you research each career thoroughly before making your choices. Don't just look at the glamorous images on the pages of the recruitment literature but read fully what each job entails. Remember that your Royal Navy career can be a long one and you need to aim for the career that is best suited to you and your circumstances. By reading all of the recruitment literature you will also be preparing yourself better for the selection process. What if you are asked the following question during the selection process: 'What do you know about your chosen career and what the job entails?' Imagine if you've only looked at the pictures and don't know what that particular job involves! It won't look good and it also demonstrates that you have not prepared yourself fully. Don't forget the importance of trying to gain some experience in your chosen trade. This can be achieved through either work experience, qualifications or simply talking to somebody who already performs a similar role.

Questions about your chosen trade to prepare for:

Q. Why have you chosen this particular trade?

Q. What can you tell me about this branch of the Royal Navy?

Q. What training is involved in order to become qualified in this branch?

Q. What equipment is used in this branch?

Q. Where is the branch based? What ship(s) and what establishment(s)?

Q. What do you expect the job to entail?

4 Practise lots of psychometric test questions

During your preparation get good at tackling psychometric test questions. During the selection process for joining the Royal Navy as a Rating you will undertake a Recruiting Test that consists of the following four areas:

- a reasoning test

- a verbal ability test

- a numerical test

- a mechanical reasoning test.

The most effective way to prepare for these tests is to carry out lots of sample test questions over a prolonged period of time. The majority of candidates will cram in their preparation the night before the test. I strongly advise against this. Use your action plan in order to build in plenty of targeted practice time.

During the actual Recruiting Test you will have a set amount of time in which to answer the questions and there will be a number of options to choose from. The tests are usually multiple choice in nature so if you find that you are running out of time towards the end of the test, take a guess! You have a one in five chance of getting it correct. You will not lose any marks for incorrect answers.

Tips to help you pass the tests

- In the build-up to the test get plenty of good quality sleep. If you are feeling tired and grouchy on the day of your test then you will not perform to your optimum ability.

- On the day before the test and also on the actual day of the test avoid caffeine and/or alcohol. Drink plenty of water so that your concentration levels are at their peak.

- If you have any special needs such as dyslexia or otherwise then be sure to inform the recruiting officer at the AFCO beforehand. They should give you more time during the test.

- If you think you've performed poorly in a particular test try to put it behind you. The Recruiting Test is just one part of the entire Royal Navy selection process and you may be able to gain better scores in the other testing areas.

- At the commencement of the test listen very carefully to the instructions and don't be afraid to ask questions if you are unsure.

- Work quickly through each of the test questions and do not spend too much time on one particular question. Let's assume that you have 15 minutes in which to answer 30 questions. On average this equates to 30 seconds per question. If you find that you are spending 40 seconds or more on some questions then you are probably taking too long, and you will run out of time before you reach the end of the test. If you are finding a question too difficult then simply leave it and move on to the next question. Be sure to leave a gap on the answer sheet for any questions that you've missed.

5 Be polite and courteous at all times, try your hardest and have the right attitude

Common courtesy and good manners are lacking in society today. You must remember that you are trying to join a disciplined service which requires you to act in a particular manner. When you apply to join the Royal Navy you will be communicating at times with experienced and professional officers. They are highly trained to pick out those people who they believe are worthwhile investments in time and money, and they will be assessing you right from the word

go. When you telephone the Armed Forces Careers Office, either to make your application or simply to arrange an informal chat I advise that you are polite and courteous at all times. General good manners such as 'good morning', 'good afternoon', 'thank you for your time' and 'please' are not as commonplace in today's society as they used to be. Being polite and courteous when communicating with the recruitment staff can help you to create the right impression right from the offset.

During my time in the Fire Service I interviewed scores of people to join the service and it was those people who were polite, respectful and courteous who grabbed my attention. First impressions are very important and if you can demonstrate a level of self-discipline before you join then this will work in your favour. Going the extra mile to make a good impression will work wonders, and it will help you to create a positive rapport with the recruitment officer.

6 Be smart and well turned out

There's an old saying: 'shiny shoes, shiny mind'. How many people do you know who clean their shoes every day? Not many I'm sure, but this can go a long way towards creating the right impression and getting you into the right frame of mind for your career in the Royal Navy. When I was preparing for my career in the Navy my father taught me how to use an iron and how to clean my shoes correctly. I can remember him showing me how to iron a shirt and a pair of trousers and initially I thought it was waste of time. However, when I joined the Royal Navy this training my father had given me proved to be invaluable. Not only did it provide me with some routine and discipline but it also forced me to take a pride in my appearance – something which is crucial to your role as a Royal Navy Rating.

Walking into the careers office with dirty shoes doesn't create a good impression. During your initial training course you will

be inspected every day on your turnout and it is far better to demonstrate to the careers officer that you have the ability to be smart before you begin your basic training. Your budget might not be big, but you can purchase a shirt and tie for little money nowadays. They don't have to be of expensive quality, but by showing that you've made an effort you will again create the right impression. If you cannot afford to buy a shirt and tie then you may be able to borrow one from a friend or relative.

It is definitely worth investing time and effort in your appearance as wearing jeans, T-shirt and trainers when attending the careers office is not going to create the right impression.

Tips for creating the right impression

- Dress smartly every time you attend the careers office.
- Make sure your shoes are cleaned and polished at all times. Get into the habit of polishing your shoes every day.
- Don't wear brightly coloured socks with your suit!
- Learn how to wear a tie correctly.

---

7 Understand the word 'teamwork' and have experience of working in a team

Do you know what the Royal Navy motto is? Yes that's right – 'The Team Works'. Why do you think the Royal Navy places such emphasis on effective teamwork? It's for the simple reason that without it, the team would fail. Think of the best football teams in the country. Those that are the most successful are not the ones that have one or two great players, but the ones that have the best overall team. The ability to work as part of a team is essential, and you will be assessed on this throughout the selection process.

As a Royal Navy Rating you will be required to work in a team environment every day in order to carry out tasks both small and large. Onboard a ship there are many different branches or men and women operating as part of individual teams that are all focused on achieving the wider team goal. Whether it is during an exercise or during warfare, your ability to work as part of a team is crucial. Although team skills will be taught during your training, you will still need to demonstrate that you have the potential to become a competent team member throughout the selection process. It is far better if you have experience of working as part of a team prior to joining the Royal Navy. If you play a form of team sports then this is even better. There are many definitions of the word 'teamwork' but the one that I believe sums it up most effectively is: *The process of working effectively with a group of people in order to achieve a goal.*

You may find in some circumstances at work, either now or in the future, where there will be people whom you dislike for various reasons. It is your ability to work with these people during difficult circumstances that makes you a good and effective team member. It is also about your ability to listen to other people's ideas and involve them in the team decisions that sets you apart from the rest. Be a team player and not an individual who knows best!

Some of the qualities of a good team player include:

- the ability to listen to others' suggestions

- being able to communicate effectively

- being capable of solving problems

- coming up with a variety of solutions to a problem

- being hard working and focused on achieving the task

- being professional and doing a good job

- helping and supporting others

- being capable of listening to a brief and having an ability to follow clear instructions.

8 Prepare effectively for the interviews

During the selection process you will be required to attend a number of interviews designed to test your suitability to join the Royal Navy. The selection officers are looking for you to demonstrate the potential and the ability to become a professional and competent Rating. I previously mentioned that first impressions are important, so during the interview you need to create the right impression, from the clothes that you wear to how you communicate and even to how you sit in the interview chair. Within this book I have dedicated an entire section to the interview and the information that I have provided you with will be a great tool during your preparation. I would estimate that I have been successful at more than 90 per cent of interviews I have attended during my career. The reason for that success is not because I am a special person but solely down to the amount of effort I put into my preparation. I always carry out a 'mock interview' before I attend the real interview and this goes a long way to helping me to succeed.

Tips for passing the interviews

- Practise a 'mock' interview. Basically this entails asking a friend or relative to interview you under formal conditions. Get them to ask you all of the interview questions that are contained within this book and try answering them.

- Prepare your responses prior to the interview. This does not mean learning the answers to the interview questions 'parrot fashion', but instead having a good idea of how you intend to respond to them.

- Concentrate on your interview technique. Sit upright in the interview chair, do not slouch, speak clearly and concisely and address the panel in an appropriate way such as 'Sir' or 'Ma'am'.

9 Practise 'deliberately' and 'repetitively' in order to improve

This next tip is an outstanding one, and one that I strongly recommend you implement during your preparation for joining the Royal Navy.

History has proven that high-performing individuals have two things in common. The first is that they deliberately identify what they are weak at, and then they go full on to improve it. The second common factor is that they repeat practising on their weak areas time and time again. Eventually, they will become outstanding at what they do. Let me give you an example. David Beckham is an outstanding footballer. He is renowned for his highly accurate crossing of the ball and free kick taking. Now, of course, David had a natural ability to play football from an early age but it wasn't this natural ability that made him so good at crossing the ball or taking free kicks. It was his 'deliberate' practice and the 'repetitive' nature of that practice that made him so good.

Before you read any further in this book I want you to think for a minute or two and write down the exact areas of the selection process that you believe you are weak at. Select your weak areas from the following list:

- 1.5-mile run

- the Royal Navy Recruiting Test

- interview technique and skills

- your knowledge of your chosen trade

- your knowledge of the Royal Navy, its history and its lifestyle

- your attitude.

Once you have identified your weak areas you then need to implement a plan that involves lots of repetitive practice. The obvious downside to continuous and repetitive practice

is that it is physically and mentally tiring. However, if you are committed to improving and reaching the peak of your abilities then the extra effort is certainly worthwhile.

Too many people give up at the first hurdle. If you realise that your fitness is not yet up to the required standard then take positive steps to improve it. If you find that your scores on the Recruiting Test are not sufficient for the career you want, then go away and practise so that the next time you take it you succeed. We all have to come face to face with hurdles or setbacks during life but it is how we deal with them that is important. Don't view failure as final. Instead, view it as an opportunity for development.

Talk to the Armed Forces Careers Office recruitment officer and ask him or her how you can improve your chances of success. Practise plenty of test questions and mock interviews, and get out there running in order to improve your fitness. I can assure you that if you pass the selection process through sheer determination and hard work you will feel a great sense of achievement that will stay with you for the rest of your life. Make success a habit.

10 Get fit for the Pre-Joining Fitness Test

Before you apply to join the Royal Navy you may already be physically active and fit but, even so, it is essential that you make your life as easy as possible. During the selection process you will need to pass the Pre-Joining Fitness Test (PJFT) which, at the time of writing, consists of a 1.5-mile run in a set time dependent on your sex and your age. The test is usually carried out at a local fitness centre or gymnasium. At the end of this book I have provided a 'How to Get Navy Fit' guide, which has been designed to assist you in your preparation. One of the most effective ways to improve your physical fitness is to embark on a structured running programme. Just by running three miles, three times a week you will be amazed at how much your fitness and general well-being will improve. Being physically fit means you will be

mentally fit too and your confidence will increase. Whatever the standard is during the selection process I advise that you aim to better it during your preparation.

When I was going through selection for the Royal Navy I forced myself to get up at 6a.m. every weekday and go for a three-mile run. It was tough, especially during the cold mornings, but I soon lost weight and got fit in the process. Getting up at 6a.m. also prepares you for your basic training. After all, you won't be able to lie in bed all morning once your training starts!

Keep trying to improve yourself and remember – be the best that you can.

THE ROYAL NAVY
RECRUITING TEST

CHAPTER 6

ABOUT THE ROYAL NAVY RECRUITING TEST

As part of the Royal Navy selection process you will be required to pass the Royal Navy Recruiting Test. The test covers the following four areas:

- a reasoning test

- a verbal ability test

- a numeracy test

- a mechanical reasoning test.

The tests are usually carried out at the Armed Forces Careers Office and will be under strict timed conditions. Details of the time restrictions and number of questions per exercise will be provided in your recruitment literature.

Within this section of the book I have provided a large number of sample test questions relating to each section to help you prepare. Please note that the questions are NOT the actual questions that you will be presented with at the test. They are a useful practice tool to help you improve your scores during

the real test. Work through each section carefully sticking to the set times. At the end of each test go back and check to see which, if any, answers you got wrong. Learning from your mistakes is a crucial part of the selection process.

CHAPTER 7
REASONING TEST

During the Royal Navy Recruiting Test you will be required to sit a reasoning test. During the test you will have 9 minutes in which to answer 30 questions.

Examples of a reasoning test question are as follows:

Sample question 1

Richard is taller than Steven. Who is shorter?

The answer in this case would be Steven as the statement indicates that Richard is taller than Steven so, therefore, Steven is the shorter of the two.

Sample question 2

Mark is not as wealthy as Jane. Who has less money?

The answer in this case would be Mark. The statement indicates that Mark is not as wealthy as Jane, implying that Jane has more money. Mark, therefore, has less money and is not as wealthy as Jane.

When you are answering this type of question it is important that you READ the question very carefully. The questions are relatively simple but they can catch you out if you do not read them properly.

Sample question 3

Car is to motorway as aeroplane is to:

A.	B.	C.	D.	E.
Sky	Wing	Holiday	Cabin crew	Sun

The answer is A – Sky. This is because a car travels on a motorway and an aeroplane travels in the sky.

Now work through the exercise on the following pages, which contains 30 sample reasoning test questions. Allow yourself 9 minutes to complete the exercise.

Once you have finished the exercise, take a look at the answers and see how well you performed. If you got any answers wrong try to understand the reason why so that can improve next time.

Reasoning test exercise 1

1. Marcus is not as bright as Andrew. *Who is brighter?*

Answer

2. Sharon is taller than Sheila. *Who is the tallest?*

Answer

3. Pauline is stronger than Beverley. *Who is the weaker of the two?*

Answer

4. Gary is lighter than Frederick. *Who is the heavier?*

Answer

5. The black car is faster than the white car. *Which car is the quickest?*

Answer

6. Rachel runs faster than her sister Georgia. *Who runs the slowest?*

Answer

7. David has more money than Arnold. *Who is the poorer?*

Answer

8. Jill is weaker than Bill. *Who is the strongest?*

Answer

9. Hayley sleeps for 10 hours and Julie sleeps for 650 minutes. *Who sleeps the longest?*

Answer

10. Sadie's shoe size is 7 and Mary's is 9. *Who needs the larger size shoes?*

Answer

11. George is sadder than Mark. *Who is the happier of the two?*

Answer

12. Pete is faster than Rick. *Who is the slowest?*

Answer

13. Jim is older than Brian. *Who is the youngest?*

Answer

14. Katie eats slower than Lucy. *Who is the faster eater?*

Answer

15. John finishes the race before Tony. *Who ran the slowest?*

Answer

16. Ink is to pen as water is to?

A.	**B.**	**C.**	**D.**	**E.**
Wash	*Fish*	*Lake*	*Drink*	*Cold*

Answer

17. Car is to drive as aeroplane is to?

A.	**B.**	**C.**	**D.**	**E.**
Holiday	*Cabin Crew*	*Airport*	*Fly*	*Wing*

Answer

18. Tall is to short as thick is to?

A.	**B.**	**C.**	**D.**	**E.**
Long	*Length*	*Line*	*Thin*	*Metre*

Answer

19. Train is to track as ship is to?

A.	**B.**	**C.**	**D.**	**E.**
Harbour	*Sea*	*Sail*	*Stern*	*Hull*

Answer

20. If the following words were arranged in alphabetical order, which one would come second?

A.	**B.**	**C.**	**D.**	**E.**
Believe	*Beast*	*Belief*	*Bereaved*	*Best*

Answer

21. If the following words were arranged in alphabetical order, which one would come last?

A.	**B.**	**C.**	**D.**	**E.**
Desire	*Desired*	*Desirable*	*Deserted*	*Desert*

Answer

22. Walk is to run as slow is to?

A.	**B.**	**C.**	**D.**	**E.**
Fast	*Speed*	*Quicker*	*Pace*	*Stop*

Answer

23. Sun is to hot as ice is to?

A.	**B.**	**C.**	**D.**	**E.**
Melt	*Winter*	*Icicle*	*Freeze*	*Cold*

Answer

24. Hammer is to nail as bat is to?

A.	**B.**	**C.**	**D.**	**E.**
Fly	*Ball*	*Cricket*	*Cat*	*Hit*

Answer

25. Book is to read as music is to?

A.	**B.**	**C.**	**D.**	**E.**
Note	*Instrument*	*Listen*	*Dance*	*Piano*

Answer

26. Which of the following words contains the most vowels?

A.	**B.**	**C.**	**D.**
Reasonable	*Combination*	*Vegetables*	*Audaciously*

Answer

27. Which of the following words contains the least vowels?

A.	**B.**	**C.**	**D.**	**E.**
Barber	*Radio*	*Disastrous*	*Elephant*	*March*

Answer

28. Chair is to sit as ladder is to?

A.	**B.**	**C.**	**D.**	**E.**
Climb	*Step*	*Bridge*	*Metal*	*Heavy*

Answer

29. Mark can run faster than Jane. Jane can run faster than Nigel who is slower than Bill. Bill runs faster than Mark. Who is the slowest?

A.	**B.**	**C.**	**D.**
Nigel	*Jane*	*Bill*	*Mark*

Answer

30. If the following words were placed in alphabetical order, which one would come third?

A.	**B.**	**C.**	**D.**
Delightful	*Delicious*	*Delayed*	*Delicate*

Answer

Now that you have completed reasoning exercise 1, take the time to work through the answers before moving on to reasoning exercise 2.

 how2become

Answers to reasoning exercise 1

1.	Andrew	11.	Mark	21.	B
2.	Sharon	12.	Rick	22.	A
3.	Beverley	13.	Brian	23.	E
4.	Frederick	14.	Lucy	24.	B
5.	The black car	15.	Tony	25.	C
6.	Georgia	16.	C	26.	D
7.	Arnold	17.	D	27.	E
8.	Bill	18.	D	28.	A
9.	Julie	19.	B	29.	A
10.	Mary	20.	C	30.	B

Reasoning test exercise 2

During the Royal Navy Recruiting Test you will find that the reasoning test may contain questions in diagrammatic format. Look at the following sample questions.

Sample question I

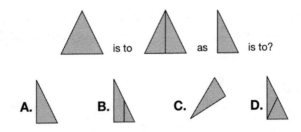

The answer is B. You will notice in the question that the straight line runs vertically through the centre of the second triangle. Therefore, the correct answer to the question is B as the straight line runs vertically through the shape.

Sample question 2

Which of the following comes next?

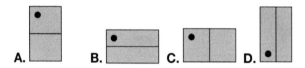

The correct answer is C. You will notice in the sample question that the black dot is moving around the shapes in a clockwise manner. It starts off in the top right-hand corner of the first shape. Then it progresses to the bottom right-hand corner of the second shape before moving round to the bottom left-hand corner of the third shape. Therefore C, where the black dot is in the top left-hand corner of the shape, is the correct answer.

Now try reasoning test exercise 2 which contains sample diagrammatic test questions. You have 9 minutes in which to answer 30 questions.

Question I

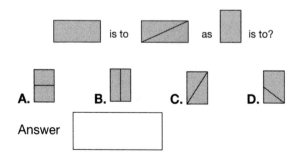

Question 2

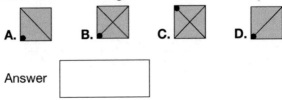

Which of the following comes next?

Answer

Question 3

Which of the following comes next?

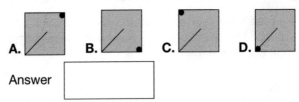

Answer

Question 4

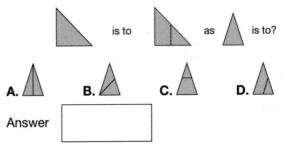

Answer

Question 5

Which of the following comes next?

A.   B.   C.   D.

Answer

Question 6

Which of the following comes next?

A.   B.   C.   D.

Answer

Question 7

is to   as   is to?

A.   B.   C.   D.

Answer

Question 8

Which of the following comes next?

A.   B.   C.   D.

Answer

Question 9

Which of the following comes next?

A.   B.   C.   D.

Answer

Question 10

   is to   as   is to?

A.   B.   C.   D.

Answer

Question II

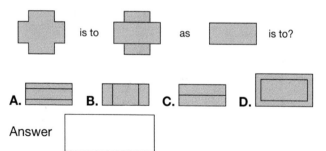

is to   as   is to?

A.   B.   C.   D.

Answer

Question I2

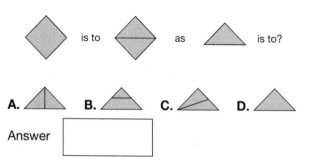

is to   as   is to?

A.   B.   C.   D.

Answer

Question I3

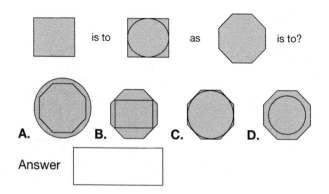

is to   as   is to?

A.   B.   C.   D.

Answer

Question 14

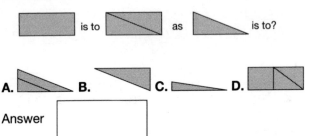

Answer [   ]

Question 15

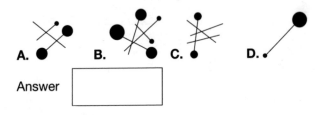

Which of the following comes next?

Answer [   ]

Question 16

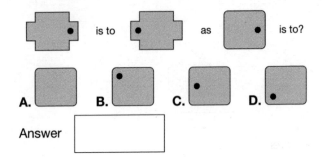

Answer [   ]

Question 17

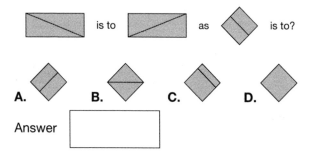

Answer

Question 18

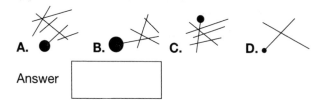

Which of the following comes next?

Answer

Question 19

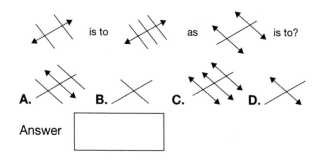

Answer

Question 20

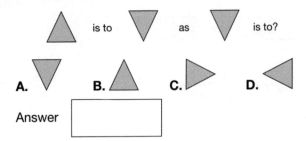

Answer

Question 21

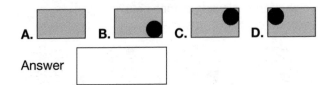

Which of the following comes next?

Answer

Question 22

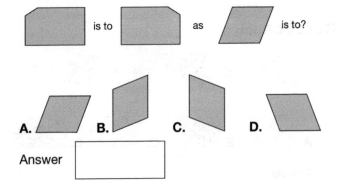

Answer

Question 23

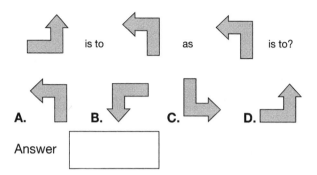

is to   as   is to?

A.   B.   C.   D.

Answer

Question 24

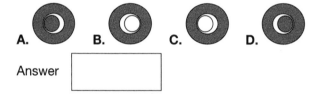

Which of the following comes next?

A.   B.   C.   D.

Answer

Question 25

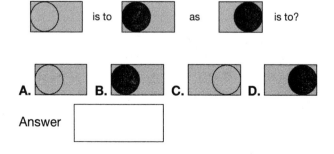

is to   as   is to?

A.   B.   C.   D.

Answer

Question 26

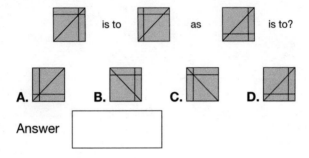

Answer [ ]

Question 27

Which of the following comes next?

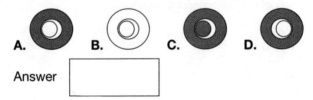

Answer [ ]

Question 28

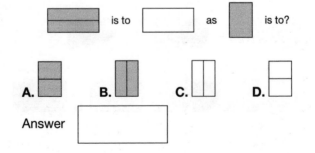

Answer [ ]

Question 29

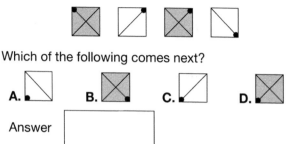

Which of the following comes next?

Answer

Question 30

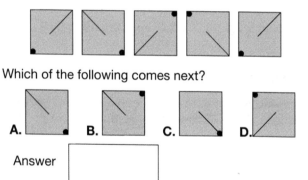

Which of the following comes next?

Answer

Now that you have completed reasoning test exercise 2 take time to work through the answers, carefully checking to see which, if any, you got wrong.

Answers to reasoning test exercise 2

1.	C	7.	C	13.	C	19.	C	25.	C
2.	B	8.	A	14.	A	20.	B	26.	A
3.	B	9.	D	15.	B	21.	C	27.	A
4.	A	10.	C	16.	C	22.	D	28.	D
5.	D	11.	A	17.	A	23.	B	29.	B
6.	C	12.	B	18.	A	24.	C	30.	A

Reasoning test exercise 3

During the Royal Navy Recruiting Test you will find that the reasoning test may contain questions in numerical format. Take a look at the following sample questions.

Sample question I

Look at the following row of numbers. Which number comes next from the options available?

16, 18, 20, 22, 24, 26, ?

A.	B.	C.	D.	E.
28	30	32	34	36

The answer is A – 28. The numbers are rising by 2 each time.

Sample question 2

Look at the following row of numbers. Which number from the options available does '?' represent?

8, 2, 10, 4, 12, 16, ?, 256

A.	B.	C.	D.	E.
8	14	16	20	24

The answer is B – 14. The 1st, 3rd and 5th numbers in the row are increasing by 2 each time which means the 7th number in the row will be 14. You will also notice that the 2nd, 4th and 6th numbers are being multiplied by themselves (e.g. $2 \times 2 = 4$, $4 \times 4 = 16$, $16 \times 16 = 256$).

Once you understand what is required in the test move on to the next exercise. There are 30 questions and you have a total of 9 minutes in which to answer them.

Question I

Look at the following row of numbers. Which number from the options available does '?' represent?

1, 3, 5, ?, 9, 11, 13

A.	B.	C.	D.	E.
6	7	8	9	10

Answer

Question 2

Look at the following row of numbers. Which number from the options available does '?' represent?

11, 12, 14, 17, 21, ?, 32

A.	B.	C.	D.	E.
22	23	24	25	26

Answer

Question 3

Look at the following row of numbers. Which number from the options available does '?' represent?

10, 25, 40, ?, 70, 85, 100

A.	B.	C.	D.	E.
35	40	45	50	55

Answer

Question 4

Look at the following row of numbers. Which number comes next from the options available?

5, 10, 10, 20, 15, 30, ?

A.	B.	C.	D.	E.
20	25	30	35	40

Answer

Question 5

Look at the following row of numbers. Which number comes next from the options available?

100, 12, 80, 14, 60, 16, ?

A.	B.	C.	D.	E.
18	20	80	40	22

Answer

Question 6

Look at the following row of numbers. Which number from the options available does '?' represent?

50, 2, 57, 4, 64, ?, 71

A.	B.	C.	D.	E.
70	78	16	85	256

Answer

Question 7

Look at the following row of numbers. Which number comes next from the options available?

3, 8, 18, 30, 70, ?

A.	B.	C.	D.	E.
150	120	110	100	90

Answer

Question 8

Look at the following row of numbers. Which number from the options available does '?' represent?

2, 4, 9, 11, 16, ?, 23

A.	B.	C.	D.	E.
17	18	19	20	21

Answer

Question 9

Look at the following row of numbers. Which number comes next from the options available?

1, 25, 4, 22, 7, 19, 10, 16, 13, ?

A.	B.	C.	D.	E.
16	15	14	13	12

Answer

Question 10

Look at the following row of numbers. Which number comes next from the options available?

5, 10, 8, 13, 14, 19, 26, 31, ?

A.	B.	C.	D.	E.
24	32	52	62	50

Answer [   ]

Question 11

Look at the following row of numbers. Which number comes next from the options available?

5, 10, 4, 11, 3, 12, ?

A.	B.	C.	D.	E.
1	13	2	14	3

Answer [   ]

Question 12

Look at the following row of numbers. Which number comes next from the options available?

90, 80, 71, 63, 56, 50, ?

A.	B.	C.	D.	E.
45	44	43	42	241

Answer [   ]

Question 13

Look at the following row of numbers. Which number from the options available does '?' represent?

?, 20, 22, 25, 29, 34, 40

A.	B.	C.	D.	E.
15	16	17	18	19

Answer

Question 14

Look at the following row of numbers. Which number from the options available does '?' represent?

?, 6, 12, 18, 24, 30, 36

A.	B.	C.	D.	E.
2	4	5	0	1

Answer

Question 15

Look at the following row of numbers. Which two numbers in order of sequence are represented by '?' from the options available?

10, 1, 15, 8, 30, 15, 45, 22, ?, ?

A.	B.	C.	D.	E.
50 + 29	50 + 19	15 + 29	60 + 29	55 + 29

Answer

Question 16

Look at the following row of numbers. Which two numbers in order of sequence are represented by '?' from the options available?

?, 11, 4, 22, 8, 33, 16, ?,

A.	**B.**	**C.**	**D.**	**E.**
2 + 44	0 + 44	2 + 32	2 + 55	= + 55

Answer

Question 17

Look at the following row of numbers. Which two numbers in order of sequence are represented by '?' from the options available?

3, 20, 6, 17, 12, 11, 21, ?, ?

A.	**B.**	**C.**	**D.**	**E.**
4 + 33	2 + 33	3 + 31	1 + 31	1 + 33

Answer

Question 18

Look at the following row of numbers. Which number comes next from the options available?

16, 20, 25, 31, 38, 46, ?

A.	**B.**	**C.**	**D.**	**E.**
52	53	54	55	56

Answer

Question 19

Look at the following row of numbers. Which number comes next from the options available?

3, 9, 27, 81, ?

A.	B.	C.	D.	E.
239	240	241	242	243

Answer

Question 20

Look at the following row of numbers. Which number comes next from the options available?

33, 35, 39, 45, 53, 63, ?

A.	B.	C.	D.	E.
75	76	77	78	79

Answer

Question 21

Look at the following row of numbers. Which number comes next from the options available?

98, 6, 92, 12, 86, 18, 80, ?

A.	B.	C.	D.	E.
76	74	70	12	24

Answer

Question 22

Look at the following row of numbers. Which number comes next from the options available?

44, 40, 40, 36, 36, 32, 32, ?

A.	**B.**	**C.**	**D.**	**E.**
22	28	30	26	24

Answer

Question 23

Look at the following row of numbers. Which three numbers in order of sequence are represented by '?' from the options available?

2, 22, ?, 20, 6, ?, 8, 16, 10, 14, ?

A.	**B.**	**C.**	**D.**
21 + 18 + 12	4 + 12 + 16	4 + 18 + 12	2 + 18 + 12

E.

2 + 16 + 12

Answer

Question 24

Look at the following row of numbers. Which number comes next from the options available?

85, 7, 80, 15, 70, 23, 55, 31, ?

A.	**B.**	**C.**	**D.**	**E.**
30	35	40	45	50

Answer

Question 25

Look at the following row of numbers. Which number comes next from the options available?

701, 202, 601, 402, 501, 602, 401, ?

A.	**B.**	**C.**	**D.**	**E.**
308	301	208	802	206

Answer

Question 26

Look at the following row of numbers. Which three numbers in order of sequence are represented by '?' from the options available?

?, ?, 6, 4, 9, 6, 12, 8, 15, ?

A.	**B.**	**C.**	**D.**
3 + 6 + 10	0 + 2 + 10	3 + 2 + 10	3 + 3 + 10

E.

3 + 2 + 18

Answer

Question 27

Look at the following row of numbers. Which number comes next from the options available?

99, 90, 91, 82, 84, 75, 78, 69, ?

A.	**B.**	**C.**	**D.**	**E.**
75	71	76	70	73

Answer

Question 28

Look at the following row of numbers. Which two numbers in order of sequence represent '?' from the options available?

?, 22, 35, 18, 39, 14, 43, 10, 47, 6, ?

A.   **B.**   **C.**   **D.**   **E.**

31 + 51   31 + 44   20 + 51   16 + 51   31 + 49

Answer [   ]

Question 29

Look at the following row of numbers. Which number comes next from the options available?

6, 12, 24, 48, 96, 192, 384, ?

A.   **B.**   **C.**   **D.**   **E.**

786   768   867   764   784

Answer [   ]

Question 30

Look at the following row of numbers. Which number comes next from the options available?

6, 9, 13, 18, 24, 31, ?

A.   **B.**   **C.**   **D.**   **E.**

35   30   40   39   49

Answer [   ]

Now that you've completed test exercise 3, work through your answers carefully rechecking which, if any, you got wrong.

Answers to reasoning test exercise 3

1. B	**9.** D	**17.** B	**25.** D
2. E	**10.** E	**18.** D	**26.** C
3. E	**11.** C	**19.** E	**27.** E
4. A	**12.** A	**20.** A	**28.** A
5. D	**13.** E	**21.** E	**29.** B
6. C	**14.** D	**22.** B	**30.** D
7. A	**15.** D	**23.** C	
8. B	**16.** A	**24.** B	

CHAPTER 8
VERBAL ABILITY TEST

During this part of the test you will be required to answer 30 questions in 9 minutes, which equates to an average of approximately 18 seconds per question. This test is designed to assess your English language skills. The test is multiple choice in nature and in the real test you will have five options to choose from. The most effective way to prepare for this type of test is to practise sample questions under timed conditions. Other ways for improving your ability include carrying out crosswords, word searches or any other tests that require an ability to work with the English language. You may also decide to purchase your own psychometric test booklet, which can be obtained from all good websites including www.how2become. co.uk.

Look at the following sample questions.

Sample question 1

Which of the following words is the odd one out?

A.	B.	C.	D.	E.
Spanner	Pliers	Hammer	Brush	Drill

The answer is D – Brush. This is because all of the other items are tools and the brush is an item used for cleaning, therefore the odd one out.

Sample question 2

The following sentence has one word missing. Which word makes the best sense of the sentence?

He had been _____ for hours and was starting to lose his concentration.

A.	B.	C.	D.	E.
studying	sleeping	complaining	walk	targeting

The correct answer is A – studying, as this word makes best sense of the sentence.

Now try verbal ability test exercise 1. There are 30 questions and you have 9 minutes in which to complete them.

Verbal ability test exercise 1

Question 1

Which of the following words is the odd one out?

A.	B.	C.	D.	E.
Car	Aeroplane	Train	Bicycle	House

Answer

Question 2

Which of the following is the odd one out?

A.	**B.**	**C.**	**D.**	**E.**
Right	White	Dart	Bright	Sight

Answer [   ]

Question 3

The following sentence has one word missing. Which word makes the best sense of the sentence?

The mechanic worked on the car for 3 hours. At the end of the 3 hours he was _____ .

A.	**B.**	**C.**	**D.**	**E.**
Home	Rich	Crying	Exhausted	Thinking

Answer [   ]

Question 4

The following sentence has two words missing. Which two words make best sense of the sentence?

The man _____ to walk along the beach with his dog. He threw the stick and the dog _____ it.

A.	**B.**	**C.**	**D.**	**E.**
hated / chose	decided / wanted	liked / chased	hurried / chased	hated / loved

Answer [   ]

how2become

Question 5

In the line below, the word outside the brackets will go with only three of the words inside the brackets to make longer words. Which ONE word will it NOT go with?

	A.	**B.**	**C.**	**D.**
In	(direct	famous	definite	cart)

Answer

Question 6

In the line below, the word outside of the brackets will go with only three of the words inside the brackets to make longer words. Which ONE word will it NOT go with?

	A.	**B.**	**C.**	**D.**
In	(decisive	reference	destructible	convenience)

Answer

Question 7

In the line below, the word outside of the brackets will go with only three of the words inside the brackets to make longer words. Which ONE word will it NOT go with?

	A.	**B.**	**C.**	**D.**
A	(float	bout	part	peck)

Answer

Question 8

Which of the following words is the odd one out?

A.	B.	C.	D.	E.
Pink	Salt	Ball	Red	Grey

Answer

Question 9

Which of the following words is the odd one out?

A.	B.	C.	D.	E.
Run	Jog	Walk	Sit	Sprint

Answer

Question 10

Which of the following words is the odd one out?

A.	B.	C.	D.	E.
Eagle	Plane	Squirrel	Cloud	Bird

Answer

Question 11

Which of the following words is the odd one out?

A.	B.	C.	D.	E.
Gold	Ivory	Platinum	Bronze	Silver

Answer

Question 12

Which of the following is the odd one out?

A.	B.	C.	D.	E.
Pond	River	Stream	Brook	Ocean

Answer

Question 13

Which of the following is the odd one out?

A.	B.	C.	D.	E.
Wood	Chair	Table	Cupboard	Stool

Answer

Question 14

Which three-letter word can be placed in front of the following words to make a new word?

time   break   light   dreamer

Answer

Question 15

Which four-letter word can be placed in front of the following words to make a new word?

box   bag   age   card

Answer

Question 16

The following sentence has one word missing. Which ONE word makes the best sense of the sentence?

After walking for an hour in search of the pub, David decided it was time to turn _____ and go back home.

A. **B.** **C.** **D.** **E.**

up in home around through

Answer

Question 17

The following sentence has one word missing. Which ONE word makes the best sense of the sentence?

We are continually updating the site and would be _____ to hear any comments you may have.

A. **B.** **C.** **D.** **E.**

pleased worried available suited scared

Answer

Question 18

The following sentence has two words missing. Which two words make the best sense of the sentence?

The Fleet Air Arm is the Royal Navy's air force. It numbers some 6,200 people, _____ is 11.5% of the _____ Royal Naval strength.

A. **B.** **C.** **D.** **E.**
which / and / which / and / which /
total total predicted corporate approximately

Answer

Question 19

The following sentence has one word missing. Which one word makes the best sense of the sentence?

The Navy has had to _____ and progress to be ever prepared to defend the British waters from rival forces.

A.   **B.**   **C.**   **D.**   **E.**

develop   manoeuvre   change   seek   watch

Answer [   ]

Question 20

Which of the following is the odd one out?

A.   **B.**   **C.**   **D.**   **E.**

Cat   Dog   Hamster   Owl   Rabbit

Answer [   ]

Question 21

Which word best fits the following sentence?

My doctor says I _____ smoke. It's bad for my health.

A.   **B.**   **C.**   **D.**   **E.**

will   wouldn't   shouldn't   like   might

Answer [   ]

Question 22

Which word best fits the following sentence?

The best thing for a hangover is to go to bed and sleep it _____ .

A.	B.	C.	D.	E.
through	over	away	in	off

Answer

Question 23

Complete the following sentence:

By the time Jane arrived at the disco, Andrew _____ .

A.	B.	C.	D.	E.
hadn't gone	already left	has already left	had stayed	had already left

Answer

Question 24

Which of the following words is the odd one out?

A.	B.	C.	D.	E.
Lawnmower	Hose	Rake	Carpet	Shovel

Answer

Question 25

Complete the following sentence:

Karla was offered the job _____ *having poor qualifications.*

A. **B.** **C.** **D.** **E.**

although   even though   with   without   despite

Answer [   ]

Question 26

Complete the following sentence:

Not only _____ *to Glasgow but he also visited many other places in Scotland too.*

A. **B.** **C.** **D.** **E.**

did she   did he   did he go   she went   she saw

Answer [   ]

Question 27

Complete the following sentence:

Now please remember, you _____ *the test until the teacher tells you to.*

A. **B.** **C.** **D.** **E.**

shouldn't   will not be   are not   can't   are not
             starting   to   start

Answer [   ]

Question 28

Which of the following is the odd one out?

A.	**B.**	**C.**	**D.**	**E.**
Strawberry	Raspberry	Peach	Blackberry	Blueberry

Answer

Question 29

Which of the following is the odd one out?

A.	**B.**	**C.**	**D.**	**E.**
Football	Wrestling	Table tennis	Golf	Rugby

Answer

Question 29

Which of the following is the odd one out?

A.	**B.**	**C.**	**D.**	**E.**
Man	Milkman	Secretary	Police Officer	Firefighter

Answer

Now that you have completed verbal ability test exercise 1, check your answers carefully before moving on to exercise 2.

Answers to verbal ability test exercise 1

1. E	5. D	9. D	13. A
2. C	6. B	10. C	14. Day
3. D	7. D	11. B	15. Post
4. C	8. D	12. A	16. D

17.	A	21.	A	25.	E	29.	B
18.	A	22.	Day	26.	C	30.	A
19.	A	23.	Post	27.	E		
20.	D	24.	D	28.	C		

Verbal ability test exercise 2

Question 1

Which one of the following words relates to the other four?

A. | **B.** | **C.** | **D.** | **E.**
Barbeque | Stove | Sausages | Burger | Cooking

Answer

Question 2

Which one of the following words relates to the other four?

A. | **B.** | **C.** | **D.** | **E.**
Television | Acting | Entertainment | Gig | Theatre

Answer

Question 3

Which one of the following words relates to the other four?

A. | **B.** | **C.** | **D.** | **E.**
Running | Fitness | Swimming | Cycling | Rowing

Answer

Question 4

Which one word inside the brackets will not go with the word outside the brackets?

Ant   (acid   agonise   eater   implode   hem)

Answer

Question 5

Which one word inside the brackets will not go with the word outside the brackets?

Tin   (stone   well   man   smith   foil)

Answer

Question 6

Which one word inside the brackets will not go with the word outside the brackets?

Band   (mess   width   wagon   leader   master)

Answer

Question 7

Which one word inside the brackets will not go with the word outside the brackets?

Grip   (ping   pier   sack   man   wool)

Ans wer

Question 8

Which one word inside the brackets will not go with the word outside the brackets?

Day   (dream   light   time   room   ball)

Answer

Question 9

Which of the following sentences has a different meaning from the other four?

A. Richard ended up buying the car for £900.

B. The car was bought by Richard for £900.

C. £900 was the amount Richard spent on the car.

D. The car cost Richard £900.

E. Richard sold the car for £900.

Answer

Question 10

Which of the following sentences has a different meaning from the other four?

A. Sally spent £350 during her shopping trip.

B. During a shopping trip Sally spent £350.

C. Sally made £350 from her shopping trip.

D. The shopping trip cost Sally £350.

E. A total of £350 was spent during Sally's shopping trip.

Answer

Question 11

Which of the following sentences has a different meaning from the other four?

A. Barry lost two stone in weight over a period of 4 months.

B. Over a 4-month period Barry gained two stone in weight.

C. Barry put on two stone in 4 months.

D. Over a period of 4 months Barry put on two stone in weight.

E. Two stone was gained in weight by Barry over a 4-month period.

Answer

Question 12

Which one of the following words relates to the other four?

A.	**B.**	**C.**	**D.**	**E.**
Cardigan	Clothes	Trousers	Shirt	Underwear

Answer

Question 13

Which one of the following words relates to the other four?

A.	**B.**	**C.**	**D.**	**E.**
Pear	Apple	Banana	Pineapple	Fruit

Answer

Question 14

Which one of the following words relates to the other four?

A.	B.	C.	D.	E.
Communicate	Email	Telephone	Speak	Letter

Answer [   ]

Question 15

Which one of the following words relates to the other four?

A.	B.	C.	D.	E.
Run	Cycle	Walk	Movement	Drive

Answer [   ]

Question 16

Which of the following sentences has a different meaning from the other four?

A. The bouncer pushed the man to the floor.

B. The man was pushed to the floor by the bouncer.

C. The bouncer was pushed by the man and he fell to the floor.

D. The bouncer pushed the man and he fell to the floor.

E. The man was pushed by the bouncer to the floor.

Answer [   ]

Question 17

Which one word inside the brackets will not go with the word outside the brackets?

Run   (around   back   charm   lets   off)

Answer

Question 18

Which one word inside the brackets will not go with the word outside the brackets?

Pot   (hole   stir   belly   ability   able)

Answer

Question 19

Which of the following is the odd one out?

A.   **B.**   **C.**   **D.**   **E.**

Apples   Parsnips Peas   Sprouts   Carrots

Answer

Question 20

Which of the following is the odd one out?

A.   **B.**   **C.**   **D.**   **E.**

Circle   Rectangle Flat   Square   Sphere

Answer

Question 21

The following sentence has one word missing. Which word makes the best sense of the sentence?

Sid _____ that he wanted to go home earlier than he originally anticipated.

A.	B.	C.	D.	E.
told	thought	boasted	decided	suddenly

Answer

Question 22

The following sentence has one word missing. Which word makes the best sense of the sentence?

Tony was often seen walking in the park with _____ dog.

A.	B.	C.	D.	E.
one	slow	his	ours	them

Answer

Question 23

The following sentence has two words missing. Which two words make the best sense of the sentence?

The album _____ *at number one in countries such as the United Kingdom and Canada, and* _____ *the charts in the United States.*

A. peaked / topped

B. eached / topped

C. got / then

D. reached / stormed

E. topped / stormed.

Answer

Question 24

The following sentence has two words missing. Which two words make the best sense of the sentence?

After four hours of looking, the _____ *for the* _____ *puppy was called off.*

A. party / search

B. search / missing

C. dog / missing

D. crying / lovely

E. puppy / lovely.

Answer

Question 25

Which of the following sentences has a different meaning from the other four?

A. He drove 80 miles to see his fiancée.

B. The man drove 80 miles so that he could see his fiancée.

C. In order to see his fiancée the man drove 80 miles.

D. After driving 80 miles the man was at last with his fiancée.

E. His fiancée had driven 80 miles to see him.

Answer

Question 26

Which of the following sentences has a different meaning from the other four?

A. It took the man five hours to complete the marathon.

B. The man completed the marathon in five hours.

C. The marathon was completed by the man in five hours.

D. Five hours later the man had completed the marathon.

E. The woman would run the marathon in five hours.

Answer

Question 27

Which one word inside the brackets will not go with the word outside the brackets?

Run   (away   day   down   over   out)

Answer

Question 28

Which one word inside the brackets will not go with the word outside the brackets?

Can   (run   teen   did   non   descent)

Answer

Question 29

The following sentence has two words missing. Which two words make the best sense of the sentence?

The boy accidentally _____ *his ball* _____ *next door's garden.*

A. accidentally / into

B. accidentally / through

C. kicked / into

D. aimed / top

E. kicked / accidentally.

Answer

Question 30

The following sentence has two words missing. Which two words make the best sense of the sentence?

It didn't _____ *the man long before he was* _____ *about the food at the restaurant again.*

A. take / complaining

B. need / asking

C. take / complimenting

D. take / eating

E. need / complaining.

Answer [ ]

Now that you have completed verbal ability test exercise 2, take the time to work through your answers carefully before moving on to the next test.

Answers to verbal ability test exercise 2

1.	E	**9.**	E	**17.**	Charm	**25.**	E
2.	C	**10.**	C	**18.**	Stir	**26.**	E
3.	B	**11.**	A	**19.**	A	**27.**	Day
4.	Implode	**12.**	B	**20.**	E	**28.**	Run
5.	Well	**13.**	E	**21.**	D	**29.**	C
6.	Mess	**14.**	A	**22.**	C	**30.**	A
7.	Wool	**15.**	D	**23.**	A		
8.	Ball	**16.**	C	**24.**	B		

CHAPTER 9
MECHANICAL COMPREHENSION TEST

During the Royal Navy Recruiting Test you will be required to sit a mechanical comprehension test that consists of 30 questions. You will have just 10 minutes in which to complete the test. Mechanical comprehension tests are an assessment that measures an individual's aptitude to learn mechanical skills. The tests are usually multiple choice in nature and present simple, frequently encountered mechanisms and situations. The majority of mechanical comprehension tests require a working knowledge of basic mechanical operations and the application of physical laws. On the following pages are a number of sample questions to help you prepare for the tests. Work through them as quickly as possible but remember to go back and check which ones you get wrong; more importantly, make sure you understand how the correct answer is reached.

In this particular exercise there are 20 questions and you have 10 minutes in which to answer them.

Mechanical comprehension test exercise 1

Question 1

If Circle 'B' turns in a clockwise direction, which way will circle 'A' turn?

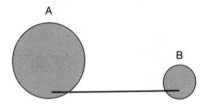

A. Clockwise

B. Anticlockwise

C. Backwards and forwards

D. It won't move

Answer

Question 2

Which square is carrying the heaviest load?

A. Square A

B. Square B

Answer

how2become

Question 3

Which pendulum will swing at the slowest speed?

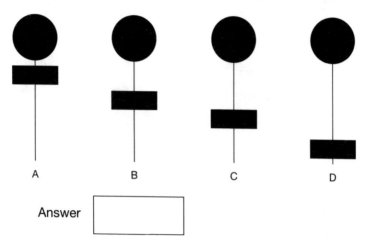

A   B   C   D

Answer

Question 4

If Cog 'A' turns in an anticlockwise direction which way will Cog 'B' turn?

A. Clockwise

B. Anticlockwise

Answer

Question 5

If Cog 'B' moves in a clockwise direction, which way will Cog 'A' turn?

A. Clockwise

B. Anticlockwise

Answer

Question 6

Which shelf can carry the greatest load?

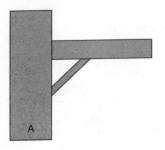
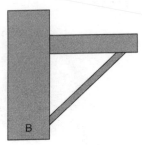

A. Shelf A

B. Shelf B

Answer

Question 7

At which point will the pendulum be travelling at the greatest speed?

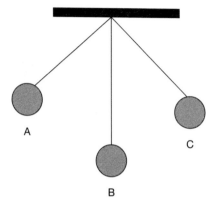

A. Point A

B. Point B

C. Point C

Answer [ ]

Question 8

At which point will the beam balance?

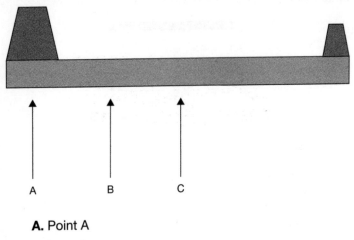

A. Point A

B. Point B

C. Point C

Answer

Question 9

If water is poured into the narrow tube, up to point 'X', what height would it reach in the wide tube?

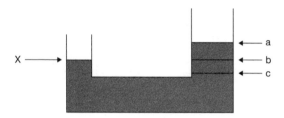

A. Point A

B. Point B

C. Point C

Answer

Question 10

At which point would Ball 'Y' have to be to balance Ball 'X'?

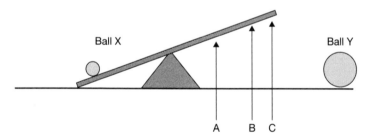

A. Point A

B. Point B

C. Point C

Answer

Question 11

If Cog 'A' turns anticlockwise, which way will Cog 'F' turn?

A. Cannot say

B. Clockwise

C. Anticlockwise

Answer

Question 12

Which post is carrying the heaviest load?

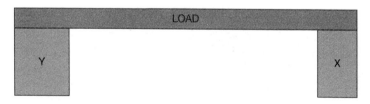

A. Both the Same

B. Post X

C. Post Y

Answer

Question 13

If water is poured in at Point D, which tube will overflow first?

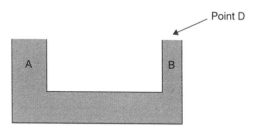

A. Tube A

B. Both the same

C. Tube B

Answer

Question 14

At which point would it be easier to haul up load X?

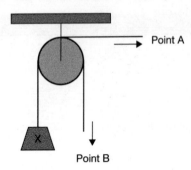

Point A

Point B

A. Both the same

B. Point A

C. Point B

Answer

Question 15

If rope 'A' is pulled in the direction of the arrow, which way will wheel 'C' turn?

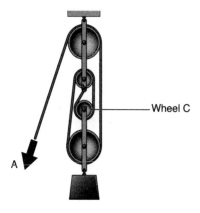

Wheel C

A

A. Clockwise

B. Anticlockwise

C. It will not turn

Answer

Question 16

Which load is the heaviest?

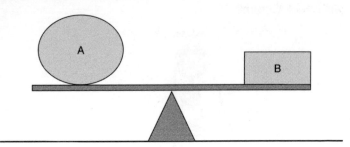

A. Both the same

B. Load B

C. Load A

Answer

Question 17

If rope 'A' is pulled in the direction of the arrow, which direction will Load 'Q' travel in?

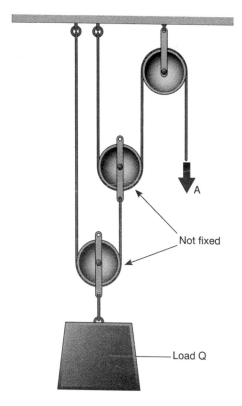

A. It will not move

B. Down

C. Up

Answer

Question 18

If circle 'X' turns anticlockwise, which way will circle 'Y' turn?

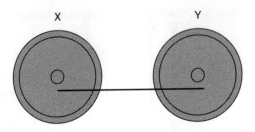

A. Anticlockwise

B. Clockwise

C. Backwards and forwards

Answer

Question 19

Which pulley system will lift the bucket of water more easily?

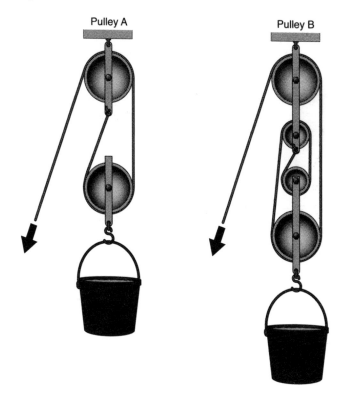

Pulley A

Pulley B

A. Both the same

B. Pulley A

C. Pulley B

Answer

Question 20

At which point(s) will the pendulum be swinging the fastest?

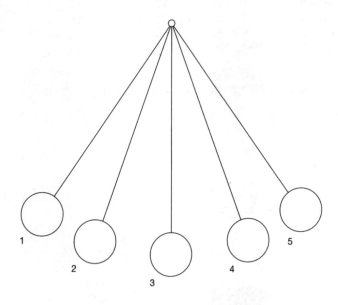

A. Point 1

B. Points 1 and 5

C. Points 3 and 5

D. Point 3

Answer

Answers to mechanical comprehension test exercise 1

1. C	**6.** B	**11.** C	**16.** C
2. B	**7.** B	**12.** C	**17.** C
3. D	**8.** B	**13.** B	**18.** A
4. B	**9.** B	**14.** A	**19.** C
5. A	**10.** A	**15.** B	**20.** D

Mechanical comprehension test exercise 2

During mechanical comprehension test exercise 2 you have 10 minutes in which to answer the 20 questions.

Question I

In the following cog and belt system, which cog will rotate the most number of times in an hour?

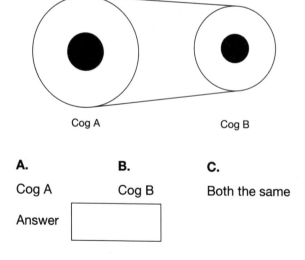

Cog A   Cog B

A.   **B.**   **C.**

Cog A   Cog B   Both the same

Answer [   ]

Question 2

In the following cog and belt system, which cog will rotate the most number of times in thirty minutes?

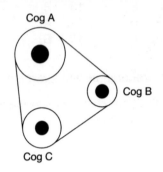

A.

Cog A

B.

Cog B

C.

Both the same

Answer

Question 3

Which rope would be the easiest to pull the mast over with?

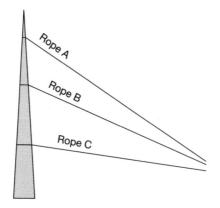

A.

Rope A

B.

Rope B

C.

Rope C

Answer

Question 4

If cog A turns anticlockwise as indicated, which way will cog C turn?

Cog C ——————   —————— Cog A

A.

Clockwise

B.

Anticlockwise

C.

Backwards
and forwards

Answer

Question 5

If cog A turns clockwise, which way will cog D turn?

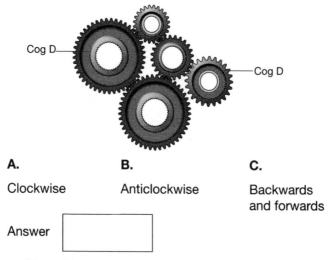

A.

Clockwise

B.

Anticlockwise

C.

Backwards
and forwards

Answer

Question 6

If wheel D moves anticlockwise at a speed of 100 rpm, how
will wheel B move and at what speed?

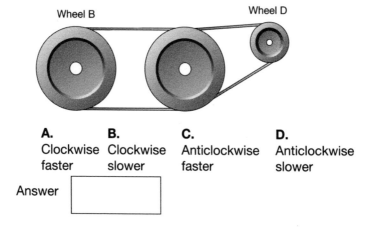

A.
Clockwise
faster

B.
Clockwise
slower

C.
Anticlockwise
faster

D.
Anticlockwise
slower

Answer

Question 7

Which is the best tool to use for tightening bolts?

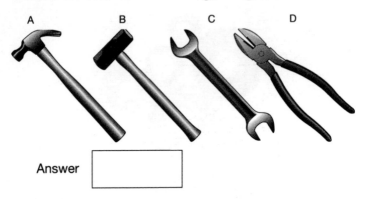

Answer

Question 8

In the following circuit, if switch A closes and switch B remains

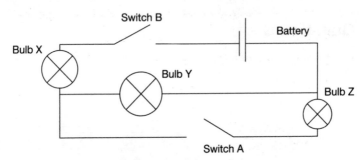

open, what will happen?

    A. Bulbs X, Y and Z will illuminate.

    B. Bulb X will illuminate only.

    C. Bulbs Y and Z will illuminate only.

    D. No bulbs will illuminate.

Answer

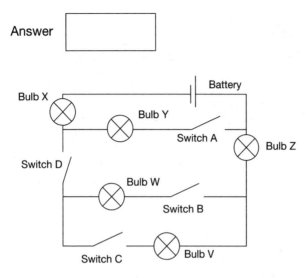

Bulb X

Bulb Y

Battery

Switch A

Bulb Z

Switch D

Bulb W

Switch B

Switch C

Bulb V

Question 9

In the following circuit, if switch A closes, what will happen?

    A. Bulbs V, W, X, Y and Z will illuminate.

    B. Bulb X and Y will illuminate only.

    C. Bulbs X, Y and Z will illuminate only.

    D. No bulbs will illuminate.

Answer

Question 10

The following four containers are filled with clean water to the same level, which is 2 metres in height. If you measured the pressure at the bottom of each container once filled with water, which container would register the highest reading? If you think the reading would be the same for each container then your answer should be E.

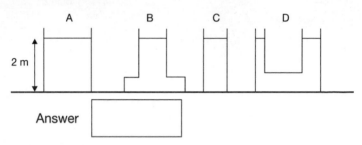

Answer

Question 11

Which of the following objects is the most unstable? If you think they are all the same then choose E for your answer.

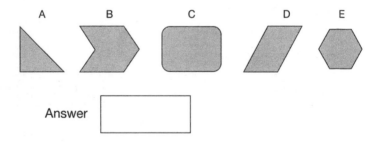

Answer

Question 12

How much weight will need to be placed at point X in order to balance out the beam?

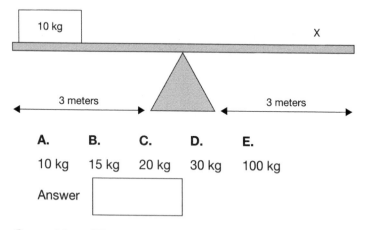

A.   **B.**   **C.**   **D.**   **E.**

10 kg   15 kg   20 kg   30 kg   100 kg

Answer

Question 13

Which post is carrying the greatest load?

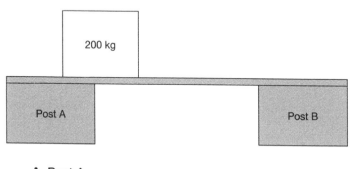

A. Post A

B. Post B

C. Both the same

Answer

Question 14

On the following weighing scales, which is the heaviest load?

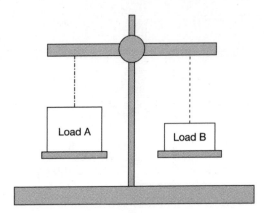

A. Load A

B. Load B

C. Both the same

Answer

Question 15

At which point should pressurised air enter the cylinder in order to force the piston downwards?

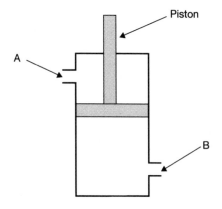

A. Point A

B. Point B

C. Both Point A and Point B

Answer

Question 16

At which point would you place the hook to keep the beam horizontal when lifted?

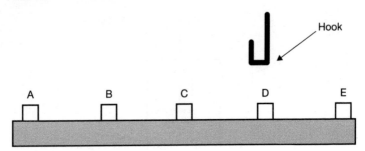

A. Point A

B. Point B

C. Point C

D. Point D

E. Point E

Answer

Question 17

At which point will the ball be travelling the fastest?

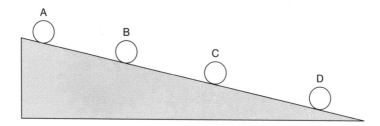

A. Point A

B. Point B

C. Point C

D. Point D

E. The same speed at each point

Answer

Question 18

If gear A moves to the right, which way will gear B move?

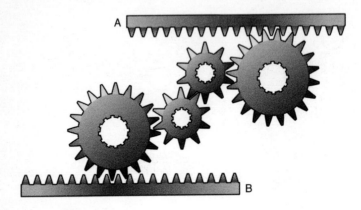

A. To the right

B. To the left

C. It won't move

D. Backwards and forwards

Answer

Question 19

At which point will the beam balance?

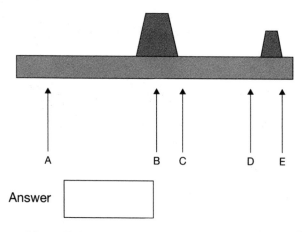

A   B   C   D   E

Answer

Question 20

Which is the heaviest load?

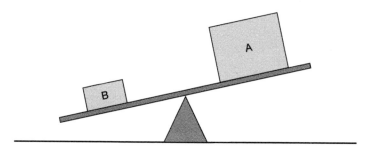

A. Load A

B. Load B

C. Both the same

Answer

Now that you have completed mechanical reasoning test exercise 2, check your answers carefully before moving on to the next test.

Answers to mechanical comprehension test exercise 2

1.	B	**6.**	D	**11.**	D	**16.**	C
2.	B	**7.**	C	**12.**	A	**17.**	D
3.	A	**8.**	D	**13.**	A	**18.**	A
4.	B	**9.**	B	**14.**	C	**19.**	C
5.	B	**10.**	E	**15.**	A	**20.**	B

CHAPTER 10
NUMERICAL REASONING TEST

During the Royal Navy Recruiting Test you will also be required to sit a numerical reasoning test. The test itself consists of 30 questions and you have 16 minutes to complete it. The most effective way to prepare for the test is to carry out plenty of practice in relation to addition, subtraction, multiplication, division and also fractions, percentages and algebra.

During the real test you won't normally be permitted to use a calculator but you will be provided with a blank sheet of paper so that you can work out your answers. Within this chapter are lots of sample test questions to help you prepare. Work carefully through the questions and be sure to check, if any, the ones you get wrong. There are 30 questions in this test and you have 16 minutes in which to answer them. Use a blank sheet of paper to work out the answers.

Numerical reasoning test exercise 1

Question I

$37 + ? = 95$

A.	B.	C.	D.	E.
85	45	58	57	122

Answer

Question 2

$86 - ? = 32$

A.	B.	C.	D.	E.
54	45	108	118	68

Answer

Question 3

$? + 104 = 210$

A.	B.	C.	D.	E.
601	314	61	106	110

Answer

Question 4

$109 \times ? = 218$

A.	B.	C.	D.	E.
1	109	12	10	2

Answer

Question 5

$6 + 9 + 15 = 15 \times ?$

A.	**B.**	**C.**	**D**	**E.**
15	2	3	4	5

Answer

Question 6

$(34 + 13) - 4 = ? + 3$

A.	**B.**	**C.**	**D.**	**E.**
7	47	51	40	37

Answer

Question 7

$35 \div ? = 10 + 7.5$

A.	**B.**	**C.**	**D.**	**E.**
2	10	4	1	17

Answer

Question 8

$7 \times ? = 28 \times 3$

A.	**B.**	**C.**	**D.**	**E.**
2	3	21	15	12

Answer

Question 9

$100 \div 4 = 67 - ?$

A.   **B.**   **C.**   **D.**   **E.**

42   24   57   333   2

Answer ☐

Question 10

$32 \times 9 = 864 \div ?$

A.   **B.**   **C.**   **D.**   **E.**

288   3   882   4   None of these

Answer ☐

Question 11

Following the pattern shown in the number sequence below, what is the missing number?

1   3   9   18   ?   72   144

A.   **B.**   **C.**   **D.**   **E.**

27   36   49   21   63

Answer ☐

Question 12

If you count from 1 to 100, how many 6s will you pass on the way?

A.   **B.**   **C.**   **D.**   **E.**

10   19   20   11   21

Answer ☐

Question 13

50% of 350 = ?

A.	**B.**	**C.**	**D.**	**E.**
170	25	175	170	700

Answer

Question 14

75% of 1000 = ?

A.	**B.**	**C.**	**D.**	**E.**
75	0.75	75000	750	7.5

Answer

Question 15

40% of 40 = ?

A.	**B.**	**C.**	**D.**	**E.**
160	4	1600	1.6	16

Answer

Question 16

25% of 75 = ?

A.	**B.**	**C.**	**D.**	**E.**
18	18.75	18.25	25	17.25

Answer

Question 17

15% of 500 = ?

A.	B.	C.	D.	E.
75	50	0.75	0.505	750

Answer

Question 18

5% of 85 = ?

A.	B.	C.	D.	E.
4	80	4.25	0.85	89.25

Answer

Question 19

9876 − 6789 = ?

A.	B.	C.	D.	E.
3078	3085	783	3086	3087

Answer

Question 20

27 × 4 = ?

A.	B.	C.	D.	E.
106	107	108	109	110

Answer

Question 21

$96 \div 4 = ?$

A.	**B.**	**C.**	**D.**	**E.**
22	23	24	25	26

Answer

Question 22

$8765 - 876 = ?$

A.	**B.**	**C.**	**D.**	**E.**
9887	7888	7890	7998	7889

Answer

Question 23

$623 + 222 = ?$

A.	**B.**	**C.**	**D.**	**E.**
840	845	740	745	940

Answer

Question 24

A rectangle has an area of 24 cm^2. The length of one side is 8 cm. What is the perimeter of the rectangle?

A.	**B.**	**C.**	**D.**	**E.**
22 inches	24 cm	18 cm	22cm	18 inches

Answer

Question 25

A square has a perimeter of 36 cm. Its area is 81cm². What is the length of one side?

A.   **B.**   **C.**   **D.**   **E.**

9 cm   18 cm   9 metres   18 metres   16 cm

Answer

Question 26

Which of the following is the same as 25/1000?

A.   **B.**   **C.**   **D.**   **E.**

0.25   0.025   0.0025   40   25000

Answer

Question 27

Is 33 divisible by 3?

A.   **B.**

Yes   No

Answer

Question 28

What is 49% of 1100?

A.   **B.**   **C.**   **D.**   **E.**

535   536   537   538   539

Answer

Question 29

One side of a rectangle is 12 cm. If the area of the rectangle is 84 cm^2, what is the length of shorter side?

A.   **B.**   **C.**   **D.**   **E.**

5 cm   6 cm   7 cm   8 cm   9 cm

Answer

Question 30

A rectangle has an area of 8 cm^2. The length of one side is 2 cm. What is the perimeter?

A.   **B.**   **C.**   **D.**   **E.**

4 cm   6 cm   8 cm   10 cm   None of these

Answer

Now that you have completed the first numerical reasoning test exercise, take the time to check through your answers carefully before moving on to exercise 2.

Answers to numerical reasoning test exercise 1

1.	C	9.	A	17.	A	25.	A
2.	A	10.	B	18.	C	26.	B
3.	D	11.	B	19.	E	27.	A
4.	E	12.	C	20.	C	28.	E
5.	B	13.	C	21.	C	29.	C
6.	D	14.	D	22.	E	30.	E
7.	A	15.	E	23.	B		
8.	E	16.	B	24.	D		

Numerical reasoning test exercise 2

There are 30 questions in this exercise and you have 16 minutes in which to answer them. Once again use a blank sheet of paper to work out the answers.

Question I

Calculate 5.99 + 16.02

A.	B.	C.	D.	E.
19.01	20.01	21.99	22.99	22.01

Answer [   ]

Question 2

Calculate 3.47 − 1.20

A.	B.	C.	D.	E.
22.7	2.27	1.27	2.67	0.27

Answer [   ]

Question 3

Calculate 98.26 − 62.89

A.	B.	C.	D.	E.
37.35	35.37	36.35	36.37	37.73

Answer [   ]

Question 4

Calculate 45.71 − 29.87

A.	**B.**	**C.**	**D.**	**E.**
14.84	18.88	14.89	15.84	15.85

Answer

Question 5

Calculate 564.87 + 321.60

A.	**B.**	**C.**	**D.**	**E.**
886.45	886.74	886.47	868.47	868.74

Answer

Question 6

Calculate 16.0 − 9.9

A.	**B.**	**C.**	**D.**	**E.**
6.9	6.1	7.1	7.9	5.1

Answer

Question 7

Calculate 1109.12 + 0.8

A.	**B.**	**C.**	**D.**	**E.**
1109.20	1109.92	1109.02	1110.20	1110.92

Answer

Question 8

Calculate 4.1 × 3.0

A.	B.	C.	D.	E.
123	9.1	12.41	7.1	12.3

Answer

Question 9

Calculate 16.8 × 4

A.	B.	C.	D.	E.
67.2	64.8	64.47	67.4	67.8

Answer

Question 10

Calculate 2.2 × 2.2

A.	B.	C.	D.	E.
4.4	44.4	2.84	4.84	8.44

Answer

Question 11

In the following equation what is the value of t?

$$\frac{5(t - 32)}{2} = 5$$

A.	B.	C.	D.	E.
64	128	43	34	39

Answer

Question 12

In the following equation what is the value of *t*?

$$\frac{3(t + 35)}{6} = 35$$

A.	B.	C.	D.	E.
35	70	75	77	30

Answer

Question 13

In the following equation what is the value of *t*?

$$\frac{9(t \times 16)}{5} = 144$$

A.	B.	C.	D.	E.
6	3	9	15	5

Answer

Question 14

In the following equation what is the value of *t*?

$$\frac{4t - 16}{32} = 2$$

A.	B.	C.	D.	E.
5	10	15	20	25

Answer

Question 15

Convert 0.7 to a fraction.

A.	B.	C.	D.	E.
$^7/_{10}$	$^3/_4$	$^{75}/_1$	$^1/_{10}$	$^2/_3$

Answer

Question 16

Convert 2.5 to a fraction.

A.	B.	C.	D.	E.
$^{25}/_1$	$^3/_6$	$2^1/_2$	$^1/_{25}$	$2^2/_1$

Answer

Question 17

Convert 3.75 to a fraction.

A.	B.	C.	D.	E.
$^{75}/_1$	$^1/_{375}$	$3^1/_{75}$	$^{75}/_3$	$3^3/_4$

Answer

Question 18

Convert $^3/_{10}$ to a decimal.

A.	B.	C.	D.	E.
3.0	0.3	3.33	0.03	0.003

Answer

Question 19

Convert ¼ to a decimal.

A.	B.	C.	D.	E.
0.025	2.5	0.25	0.4	4.0

Answer

Question 20

Convert ⅘ to a decimal.

A.	B.	C.	D.	E.
0.08	8.0	4.5	5.4	0.8

Answer

Question 21

60 × 0.25 = ?

A.	B.	C.	D.	E.
125	20	15	10	5

Answer

Question 22

The clock below reads 10:10a.m. How many degrees will the large (minute) hand have turned when the time reaches 11:10a.m?

A.   **B.**   **C.**   **D.**   **E.**

60°   360°   90°   180°   12°

Answer

Question 23

The clock below reads 10:10a.m. How many degrees will the large (minute) hand have turned when the time reaches 10:55a.m?

A.	B.	C.	D.	E.
45°	360°	90°	180°	270°

Answer

Question 24

The clock below reads 10:10a.m. How many degrees will the small (hour) hand have turned when the time reaches 4:10p.m?

A.   **B.**   **C.**   **D.**   **E.**

60°   360°   90°   180°   270°

Answer

Question 25

220 × 0.75 = ?

A.   **B.**   **C.**   **D.**   **E.**

110   180   200   160   165

Answer

Question 26

What is the number 67.987651 correct to 3 decimal places?

A.	**B.**	**C.**	**D.**	**E.**
67.988	68	67.987	67.9	67.98

Answer

Question 27

What is the number 88.88087 correct to 2 decimal places?

A.	**B.**	**C.**	**D.**	**E.**
89.0	89.9	88.90	88.88	89.88

Answer

Question 28

$550 \times 0.2 = ?$

A.	**B.**	**C.**	**D.**	**E.**
110	100	50	55	275

Answer

Question 29

$1100 \times 0.3 = ?$

A.	**B.**	**C.**	**D.**	**E.**
90	300	990	330	310

Answer

Question 30

890 × 0.4 = ?

A.	B.	C.	D.	E.
890.4	356	8904	365	445

Answer

Now that you have completed numerical reasoning test exercise 2 take the time to carefully work through your answers. Make sure you learn from any mistakes you made.

Answers to numerical reasoning test exercise 2

1.	E	**9.**	A	**17.**	E	**25.**	E
2.	B	**10.**	D	**18.**	B	**26.**	A
3.	B	**11.**	D	**19.**	C	**27.**	D
4.	D	**12.**	A	**20.**	E	**28.**	A
5.	C	**13.**	E	**21.**	C	**29.**	D
6.	B	**14.**	D	**22.**	B	**30.**	B
7.	B	**15.**	A	**23.**	E		
8.	E	**16.**	C	**24.**	D		

CHAPTER II
TIPS FOR PASSING THE ROYAL NAVY RECRUITING TEST

- In the build-up to the test make sure you get in plenty of practice in the assessable areas.

- Carry out 'deliberate' and 'repetitive' practice and work hard on your weak areas in order to improve.

- Practise under timed conditions and without the aid of a calculator. Use a blank sheet of paper to work out your calculations.

- If you find that you are struggling to pass or understand the practice tests then consider getting some personal tuition or help.

- Drink plenty of water in the build-up to the tests in order to maintain your concentration levels.

- Practise little and often as opposed to 'cramming' the night before the test.

 how2become

CHAPTER 11

TIPS FOR PASSING
THE ROYAL NAVY
RECRUITING TEST

THE ROYAL NAVY
SELECTION INTERVIEW

CHAPTER 12

HOW TO PASS THE ROYAL NAVY SELECTION INTERVIEW

During the Royal Navy selection process you will be required to sit a number of interviews depending on the choice of career you make. The interviews are usually held at your local Armed Forces Careers Office and will be undertaken by a member of the Royal Navy recruitment team. The duration of the interview will very much depend on your responses to the questions. However, you can expect the interview to last for approximately 30 minutes. The questions that you will be assessed against during the initial interview will normally be taken from the following areas:

- The reasons why you want to join the Royal Navy and why you have chosen this service over the Army and the Royal Air Force.

- What choice of career you are most interested in, the reason for choosing that career, and the skills you have to match the role.

- What you already know about the Royal Navy, its history, its lifestyle and training.

- Your hobbies and interests including sporting/team activities.

- Any personal responsibilities that you currently have at home, in your education or at work.

- Your family and your partner and what they think about you joining.

- Information you gave in your initial application.

- Your experience of work and education.

- Your emotional stability and your maturity.

- Your drive and determination to succeed.

- Your reaction to a disciplined environment and attitude towards people in positions of authority.

Before I move on to a number of sample interview questions and responses I want to explain a little about interview technique and how you can come across in a positive manner during the interview. During my career in the Fire Service I sat on many interview panels assessing people who wanted to become a firefighter. As you can imagine there were some good applicants and there were also some poor ones. Let me explain the difference between a good applicant and a poor one.

A good applicant

A good applicant is someone who has taken the time to prepare. They have researched both the organisation they are applying to join and also the role that they are being interviewed for. They may not know every detail about the organisation and the role but it will be clear that they have made an effort to find out important facts and information. They will be well presented at the interview and they will be

confident, but not overconfident. As soon as they walk into the interview room they will be polite and courteous and they will sit down in the interview chair only when invited to do so. Throughout the interview they will sit upright in the chair and communicate in a positive manner. If they do not know the answer to a question they will say so and they won't try to waffle. At the end of the interview they will ask positive questions about the job or the organisation before shaking hands and leaving.

A poor applicant

A poor applicant could be any combination of the following. They will be late for the interview or even forget to turn up at all. They will have made little effort to dress smartly and they will have carried out little or no preparation. When asked questions about the job or the organisation they will have little or no knowledge. Throughout the interview they will appear to be unenthusiastic about the whole process and will look as if they want the interview to be over as soon as possible. While sitting in the interview chair they will slouch and fidget. At the end of the interview they will try to ask clever questions that are intended to impress the panel.

Earlier in the book I made reference to a 'mock interview'. I strongly advise that you try out a mock interview before the real thing. You'll be amazed at how much your confidence will improve. All you need to do is get your parents or a friend to sit down with you and ask you the interview questions that are contained within this guide. Answer them as if you were at the real interview. The more mock interviews you try the more confident you'll become.

Interview technique

How you present yourself during the interview is important. While assessing candidates for interviews I will not only assess their responses to the interview questions but I will also pay attention to the way they present themselves. A candidate could give excellent responses to the interview questions but if they present themselves in a negative manner this could lose them marks.

Take a look at the diagrams below which indicate both poor technique and good technique.

Poor interview technique

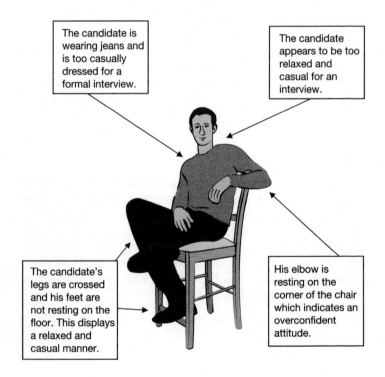

The candidate is wearing jeans and is too casually dressed for a formal interview.

The candidate appears to be too relaxed and casual for an interview.

The candidate's legs are crossed and his feet are not resting on the floor. This displays a relaxed and casual manner.

His elbow is resting on the corner of the chair which indicates an overconfident attitude.

Good interview technique

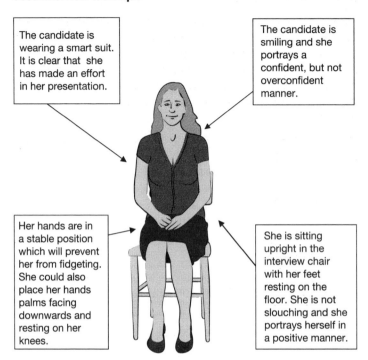

The candidate is wearing a smart suit. It is clear that she has made an effort in her presentation.

The candidate is smiling and she portrays a confident, but not overconfident manner.

Her hands are in a stable position which will prevent her from fidgeting. She could also place her hands palms facing downwards and resting on her knees.

She is sitting upright in the interview chair with her feet resting on the floor. She is not slouching and she portrays herself in a positive manner.

In the build-up to your interview practise a few mock interviews. Look to improve your interview technique as well as working on your responses to the interview questions.

Now let's look at a number of sample interview questions. Please note that these questions are not guaranteed to be the exact ones you'll be asked at the real interview but they are a great starting point in your preparation. Use the sample responses that I have provided as a basis for your own preparation. Construct your answers based on your own opinions and experiences.

Sample interview questions and responses

Sample interview question 1

Why do you want to join the Royal Navy?

This is an almost guaranteed question during the selection interview so there should be no reason why you can't answer it in a positive manner. Only you will know the real reason why you want to join, but consider the following benefits before you construct your response:

- A career in the Royal Navy is challenging. You will face challenges that are not usually available in normal jobs outside of the Armed Forces. These challenges will make you a better person and they will develop you into a professional and competent member of a proud organisation.

- A career in the Royal Navy will not only give you the chance to develop your skills and potential but it will also give you a trade.

- A career in the Royal Navy will give you the chance to travel and see different cultures. This alone will broaden your horizons and make you a more rounded person.

- The Royal Navy, like the other Armed Forces, is an organisation for which people have a huge amount of respect. Therefore, those people who join it are very proud to be a part of such a team.

Display a good level of motivation when answering questions of this nature. The Royal Navy is looking for people who want to become a professional member of its team and who understand its way of life. It should be your own decision to join and you should be attracted to what this career has to offer. If you have been pushed into joining by your family then you shouldn't be there! Below is a sample response to this question.

Sample response to interview question 1

Why do you want to join the Royal Navy?

I have been working towards my goal of joining the Royal Navy for a number of years now. A couple of years ago a careers adviser visited our school to talk about the Navy. After his presentation I went up to him and asked a few questions about the different career options that were available. Since that day I have set my sights on joining this organisation and I have been working hard to improve myself. To be honest, I want a career that will give me direction, professional training and the chance to work with people who set themselves very high standards. I have spoken to a friend who already works in the Navy as a steward and he fully recommends it.

I've looked at the different career options outside of the Royal Navy and nothing matches up to the challenge or the sense of pride I would feel by joining a team like this. I play rugby at my school and being part of a winning team is something that I very much enjoy. Even though I am quite capable of working on my own I much prefer to work in a team where everyone is working towards the same goal.

Finally, even though I have a good stable home life I can't wait to leave home and see what's out there. Even though travelling isn't the be all and end all I am looking forward to visiting different countries and experiencing different cultures. Many of my friends have never been out of their home town but that's not for me. I want to broaden my skills and get some decent training in the process and I believe that I would be a great asset to the Royal Navy.

Sample interview question 2

Why have you chosen the Royal Navy over the Army or the Royal Air Force?

As you know, there are three main forces that you can apply to join. The Navy is different from the other forces in the way

that you'll be required to serve onboard ship for many months of your career. To some, this is not appealing. Personally, I enjoyed my time onboard ship. I spent my time in the Fleet Air Arm which meant that I didn't spend half as much time onboard ship as the other branches of the Royal Navy. Other branches will live onboard ship 365 days a year, even when it is dockside. You need to be fully comfortable with this fact and be 100 per cent certain that you can cope with the demands of living on a ship. I believe there is nothing better than being onboard ship, and when you arrive back home after a long trip it makes you appreciate your home soil even more.

The Royal Navy will give you so much variety and it will also give you many different career options. The amount of activity, skills and experience that I crammed into my Royal Navy career was unbelievable. You won't get that in any other job!

Look at the following sample response to this question before creating your own based on your views and opinions.

Sample response to interview question 2

Why have you chosen the Royal Navy over the Army or the Royal Air Force?

I did consider the other forces and even had a chat with each of the careers advisers but in the end I was still set on the Royal Navy. I even sat down with my parents and we wrote down the benefits of each of the different services and the Royal Navy came out on top in all aspects. I have always had a keen passion to work on aircraft and I also would like to travel. The Fleet Air Arm is my first choice because I would get to work onboard ship in addition to working on aircraft. During my research I visited the Fleet Air Arm museum at HMS Heron and I was fascinated with the history and the aircraft that have formed part of the service over the years.

I have thought long and hard about my choice of career and I am fully aware of the training that I will undergo if I

am successful. I've been working hard to pass the selection process and am 100 per cent certain that the Royal Navy is for me. If I am unsuccessful at this attempt then I will look at what I need to improve on and work hard for next time.

Sample interview question 3

What does your family think of you wanting to join the Royal Navy?

What the members of your family think about you wanting to join the Royal Navy is very important, simply for the reason that you will need their support both during your training and during your career. I can remember my parents being fully behind my decision to join the Royal Navy and I'm glad that they were for a very good reason. After about two weeks into my basic training I started to feel a little bit homesick, like any young man would do being away from home for a long period of time. I rang my father and discussed with him how I felt. After about five minutes' chat on the phone I felt perfectly fine and no longer homesick. During that conversation he reminded me how hard I had worked to get a place on the course and that he and my mother wanted me to succeed. For that reason alone I was glad that I had the support of my parents.

Before you apply to join the Royal Navy it is important that you discuss your choice of career with either your parents or your guardian. If you have a partner then obviously you will need to discuss this with them too. If they have any concerns whatsoever then I would advise you to take them along with you to the Armed Forces Careers Office so they can discuss these concerns with the trained recruitment staff. Get their full support as you may need it at some point during your career, just like I did.

Below is a sample response to help you prepare.

Sample response to interview question 3

What does your family think of you wanting to join the Royal Navy?

Before I made my application I discussed my choice of career with both my parents and my girlfriend. Initially they were apprehensive but they could see how motivated and excited I was as I explained everything I had learnt so far about the service. I showed them the recruitment literature and we even planned a trip to the Fleet Air Arm museum so they could see what I would be joining. I understand that it is important they support me during my application and I now have their full backing. In fact, they are now more excited about the fact I'll be leaving home than I am! I have also told them everything I know about the training I will go through and the conditions I will serve under. They are aware that the Royal Navy has a brilliant reputation and this has helped them to understand further why I want to join. We also spent time looking at the Royal Navy website on the section that is for parents and they can see fully the benefits that this career will have for me. They are also looking forward to hopefully seeing me at my passing out parade if I am successful and, therefore, I have their full backing.

Sample interview question 4

What grades did you achieve at school and how do you feel about them?

Questions that relate to your education are common during the selection interview. In addition to this question they may also ask you questions that relate to which schools or educational establishments you attended.

This kind of question is designed to assess your attitude to your grades and also how hard you worked while at school. As you can imagine, your grades will generally reflect how hard you worked and, therefore you will need to be totally honest in your response. If, like me, you achieved very few

educational qualifications then you will need to explain what you intend to do about it in the future. Despite leaving school with few GCSEs it was later on in my life that I really started to realise my academic potential. While waiting for my start date when I joined the Navy I went back to college and embarked on a foundation course to improve my grades. If you achieved the grades you wanted during education then congratulations, you'll find this question easier to answer.

Look at the following sample response which is based on my own circumstances at the time of joining.

Sample response to interview question 4

What grades did you achieve at school and how do you feel about them?

To be totally honest I didn't do as well as I had hoped. The reason for this was that I didn't work hard enough during the build-up to the exams. I'd put in some preparation but I now realise I should have worked harder. In order to improve my grades I have decided to embark on a foundation course at my local college and I start this in a month's time. In the build-up to selection I have been working hard on my academic abilities and know that I can do well on the written tests. I've certainly learnt from my lack of educational qualifications and I can assure you that if I am successful I will be working extremely hard to pass all of my exams during both my basic training and my branch training.

Sample interview question 5

What responsibilities do you have either at work, school or at home?

When you join the Royal Navy you will need to take responsibility not only for yourself, but also for your kit, your equipment and for the safety of your work colleagues. At the age of 18 I was responsible for servicing and maintaining Sea

Harrier jets on board HMS *Invincible*. I was responsible for going out on deck at 4a.m. and servicing the ejector seats that formed part of the pilot's safety equipment. That's a huge amount of responsibility to undertake. Whatever branch you decide to join you will need to demonstrate during selection that you can handle responsibility. The most effective way to do this is by providing the interviewer with examples of when you have already held positions of responsibility either at home, work or during your education.

Look at the following sample response to this question.

Sample response to interview question 5

What responsibilities do you have either at work, school or at home?

I currently hold a few responsibilities both at home and in my part-time job. I'm responsible for cleaning the house top to bottom once a week and I usually do this on a Sunday before I play football for my local team. I'm also Captain of my football team which means I have to arrange the fixtures and book the football ground. I also collect the kit at the end of the match, and get it washed and dried for the following week's fixture.

I have just started a new job at my local supermarket where I'm responsible for serving customers and making sure stock levels are kept up. This involves cross-checking current stock levels with required standards and I have to report daily to my manager with any discrepancies or missing items or goods. While serving the customers I'm responsible for ensuring I give them a good level of service and I also have to check people for identification if they appear to be under the required age to purchase alcohol or cigarettes.

I enjoy taking on responsibility as it gives me a sense of achievement. I understand that I will need to be responsible during my Royal Navy training not only for the upkeep of my kit and equipment but I'll also have to make sure I am

punctual and that I make the time to study hard in the evening for my exams.

Sample interview question 6

How do you think you will cope with the discipline, regimentation and routine in the Royal Navy?

When you join the Navy you will be joining a military organisation that has set procedures, standards and discipline codes. Procedures, standards and discipline codes are there for a very good reason. They ensure that the organisation operates at its optimum best and without them things would go wrong, and people would either be injured or at worst killed. To some people these important aspects of service life will come as a shock when they join. The recruitment staff will want to know that you are fully prepared for this change in lifestyle. They are investing time, effort and resources into your training so they want to know that you can cope with their way of life.

When answering this type of question you need to demonstrate both your awareness of what Royal Navy life involves and also your positive attitude towards the disciplined environment. Study the recruitment literature and visit the careers website to get a feel for the type of training you will be going through. Below is a sample response to this question.

Sample response to interview question 6

How do you think you will cope with the discipline, regimentation and routine in the Royal Navy?

I believe I would cope with it very well. In the build-up to selection I have been trying to implement routine and discipline into my daily life. I've been getting up at 6a.m. every weekday morning and going on a three-mile run. This will hopefully prepare me for the early starts that I'll encounter during training. I've also been learning how to iron my own clothes

and I've been helping around the house with the cleaning and washing, much to the surprise of my parents!

I fully understand that the Navy needs a disciplined workforce if it is to function as effectively as it does. Without that discipline things could go wrong and if I did not carry out my duties professionally then I could endanger somebody's life. For example, I want to become a Marine Engineer which is an extremely responsible job. If I did not carry out my job correctly and also look after my tools and equipment then I would not only be failing in my duty, but I would also be endangering other people's lives. I fully understand why discipline is required and believe I would cope with it well. I understand that being in the Navy isn't a nine-to-five job but instead you have to take on tasks whenever required.

I have read all of the recruitment literature and I know there are people from every background working in the team. I know that I can bring something to the team too.

Sample interview question 7

How do you think you will cope with being away from home and losing your personal freedom?

This type of question is one that needs to be answered positively. The most effective way to respond to it is to provide the recruitment staff with examples of when you have already lived away from home for a period of time. This could be either with your school or college, an adventure trip, camping with friends or even with a youth organisation. Think of occasions when you have had to fend for yourself or even 'rough it' during camps or adventure trips. If you are already an active person who spends very little time sitting at home in front of the television or computer, then you will probably have no problem with losing your personal freedom. During your time in the Navy there'll be very little opportunity to sit around doing nothing anyway. So, if you're used to being active before you join, this is a plus.

Take a look at the sample response below and try to structure your own response around this.

Sample response to interview question 7

How do you think you will cope with being away from home and losing your personal freedom?

I already have some experience of being away from home so I believe I would cope quite well. While serving with the Sea Cadets I was introduced to the Navy way of life and I fully understand what it is like to be away from home. Having said that, I am not complacent and I have been working hard to improve my fitness and academic skills. To be honest with you, I'm not the kind of person who sits around at home watching television or using the computer, so I'm hardly indoors anyway. In terms of losing my personal freedom I'm looking forward to the routine and regimentation that the Navy will provide as I believe this will bring some positive structure to my life. Even though I am young I want to ensure that I have a good future and I believe a career in the Royal Navy will bring me just that, providing that is, I work hard during training.

During my time in the Sea Cadets I've been away on a couple of camps and I really enjoyed this. We learnt how to fend for ourselves and I loved the fact that I was meeting new and interesting people. I understand that the training will be difficult and intense but I am fully prepared for this. I am confident that I will cope with the change in lifestyle very well.

Sample interview question 8

Are you involved in any sporting activities and how do you keep yourself fit?

During the selection interview you will be asked questions that relate to your sporting activities and how you keep yourself fit.

If you are the type of person who spends too much time using the computer or social networking sites then now's the time to make a positive change. Remember our action plan? You can add positive structure to your life and implement some form of sporting activity or fitness regime. Even though you'll be onboard ship there will still be time for sporting activities. While onboard HMS *Invincible* I really got into my weight training. Right at the bottom of the ship there was a small gym, and even though it was usually packed full of Royal Marines, there was still time to keep fit. On the odd occasion when the flight deck wasn't being used for flying operations it was opened up for running and general sports such as volleyball. All of these helped to keep up the team morale onboard ship.

Sample response to interview question 8

Are you involved in any sporting activities and how do you keep yourself fit?

I am an extremely fit and active person and I am currently involved in a couple of sports teams. To begin with, I visit the gym four times a week and carry out a light weight session before swimming half a mile in the pool. Sometimes I like to vary the gym session with a workout on the indoor rowing machine. In the build-up to selection I have been getting up at 6a.m. every weekday and going on a three-mile run. This, I believe, will prepare me for the early starts during selection.

I am also a member of my local hockey team and I practise with them one evening a week during the season. We usually play one match a week which forms part of a Sunday league table. We are currently third in the table and are pushing hard for the top spot.

Finally, I am a keen hill walker and love to take off for long walks in the Lake District or Brecon Beacons with some of my friends. We usually camp out for a couple of nights over a weekend so I am used to fending for myself. I am not the type

of person who just sits at home on the computer or playing video games. I love being active and always keep myself fit.

Sample interview question 9

What do you think are the qualities of a good team player?

Remember the Royal Navy motto 'The team works'? I have already made reference to the importance of teamwork during this book and there is a possibility that you will be asked a question that relates to your ability to work as part of a team and also what you think are the qualities of an effective team worker. While onboard ship there is a high risk that things can go wrong. You are hundreds of miles away from land and any support from other ships could be hours away. If something serious goes wrong then you have to work very fast and professionally as part of a team in order to resolve the issue. Before you can work effectively as a team, however, you need to know what the main qualities of a competent team member include.

- An ability to interact and work with others, regardless of their age, sex, religion, sexual orientation, background, disability or appearance.

- Being able to communicate with everyone in the team and provide the appropriate level of support and encouragement.

- Being capable of carrying out tasks correctly, professionally and in accordance with guidelines and regulations.

- Being focused on the team's goal(s).

- Having a flexible attitude and approach to the task.

- Putting the needs of the team first before your own.

- Putting personal differences aside for the sake of the team.

- Being able to listen to others' suggestions and contributions.

When responding to this type of question it would be an advantage if you could back up your response with an example of where you already work in a team. Look at the following sample response before creating your own based on your experiences and ideas.

Sample response to interview question 9

What do you think are the qualities of a good team player?

A good team player must have many different qualities including an ability to listen carefully to a given brief. If you don't listen to the brief that is provided then you can't complete the task properly. In addition to listening carefully to the brief you must be able to communicate effectively with everyone in the team. This will include providing support for the other team members and also listening to other people's suggestions on how a task can be achieved. You also have to be able to work with anyone in the team regardless of their age, background, religion, sexual orientation, disability or appearance. You can't discriminate against anyone and if you do, then there is no place for you within that team. A good team player must also be able to carry out his or her job professionally and competently. When I say competently I mean correctly and in accordance with guidelines and training. You should also be focused on the team's goal and not be distracted by any external factors. Putting the needs of the team first is paramount. Finally, a good team player must be flexible and be able to adapt to the changing requirements of the team.

I already have some experience of working in a team and I know how important it is to work hard at achieving the task. I have a part-time job at weekends working in my local supermarket and every week we have a team briefing. During the team briefings my manager will inform us what jobs need to be carried out as a priority. During one particular meeting he asked three of us to clear a fire escape that had become blocked with cardboard boxes, debris and rubbish. He also

asked us to come up with a plan to prevent it from happening again. We quickly set about the task, carefully removing the rubbish, and I had the responsibility of arranging for a refuse collection company to come and dispose of the rubbish. We also had to work together to find ways of preventing the rubbish from being haphazardly dumped in the same way again in the future. We sat down together and wrote out a memorandum for our manager that he could distribute to all staff. At the end of the job we'd worked well to achieve the task and no more rubbish was ever dumped in the fire escape again. My manager was very pleased with the job we'd done.

Sample interview question 10

What do you do in your spare time?

Questions of this nature are designed to assess how effectively you use your spare time. If you are an inactive person who sits indoors watching television most days you are less likely to adapt to the change in lifestyle the Navy will bring than if you are a fit, active and sporty type of person.

Positive ways to spend your spare time

- Brisk walking, running, gym work, swimming, cycling, indoor rowing.

- Studying for exams or academic qualifications.

- Preparing for a goal or aspiration such as joining the Royal Navy.

- Team activities such as football, hockey, rugby.

- Outdoor activities such as mountaineering, orienteering, mountain biking or climbing.

- Charity or voluntary work.

Negative ways to spend your spare time

- Sitting at home watching television or playing computer games.
- Spending hours on social networking sites.
- Sitting on park benches or being on the streets doing nothing.

Take a look at the box below which differentiates between positive ways to spend your spare time and negative ways.

Now look at the following sample response to this question which will assist you in your preparation.

Sample response to interview question 10

What do you do in your spare time?

During my spare time I like to keep active, both physically and mentally. I enjoy visiting the gym three times a week and I have a structured workout that I try to vary every few months to keep my interest up. When I attend the gym I like to work out using light weights and I also enjoy using the indoor rower. I always try to beat my best time over a 2000-metre distance.

I'm also currently doing a weekly evening class in Judo, which is one of my hobbies. I haven't achieved any grades yet but I am taking my first one in a few weeks' time. I'm also a member of the Sea Cadets, which is an evening's commitment every week and the occasional weekend. Of course, I know when it is time to relax and usually do this by either listening to music or playing snooker with my friends but, overall, I'm quite an active person. I certainly don't like sitting around doing nothing. I understand that if I'm successful in joining the Navy then there will be lots to keep me occupied in the evenings, especially during my basic training.

Sample interview question II

Can you tell me about any achievements you have attained during your life so far?

Those people who can demonstrate a history of achievement during the Royal Navy interview are far more likely to pass the initial training course. Demonstrating a history of achievement will work in your favour. Having achieved something in your life demonstrates that you have the ability to see things through to the end, something which is crucial to your career in the Navy. It also shows that you are motivated and determined to succeed.

Think of examples where you have succeeded or achieved something relevant in your life. Some good examples of achievements are as follows:

- Winning a trophy with a football or hockey team.

- GCSEs and other educational qualifications.

- Duke of Edinburgh's Award.

- Being given responsibility at work or at school.

- Raising money for charity.

Obviously you will include your own achievements in your response, but below is an example. Once you have read it, think of occasions in your life when you have achieved something of importance.

Sample response to interview question 11

Can you tell me about any achievements you have attained during your life so far?

Yes I can. So far in my life I have achieved quite a few things that I am proud of. To begin with, I achieved good grades while at school including a grade 'A' in English. I worked very hard to achieve my grades and I'm proud of them. At

weekends I play rugby for a local team and I've achieved a number of things with them. Apart from winning the league last year we also held a charity match against the local police rugby team. We managed to raise £500 for a local charity which was a great achievement.

More recently, I managed to achieve a huge increase in my fitness levels in preparation for the Pre-Joining Fitness Test. Before I started my preparation I couldn't reach the minimum standard required, but I have since worked vary hard and I can now easily pass the required target for my age group.

Sample interview question 12

What are your strengths and what are you good at?

This is a common interview question that is relatively easy to answer. The problem with it is that many people use the same response. It is quite an easy thing to tell the interviewer that you are dedicated and the right person for the job. However, it is a different thing backing it up with evidence!

If you are asked this type of question make sure you are positive during your response and show that you actually mean what you are saying. Then, back up the strengths you have mentioned with examples of when you have been something that you say you are. For example, if you tell the panel that you are a motivated person, back it up with an example in your life when you have achieved something through sheer motivation and determination.

Below is a sample response to this type of question.

Sample response to interview question 12

What are your strengths and what are you good at?

To begin with, I'm a determined person who likes to see things through to the end. For example, I recently ran a marathon for charity. I'd never done this kind of thing before and found

it very hard work, but I made sure I completed the task. Another strength of mine is that I'm always looking for ways to improve myself. As an example, I have been preparing for the Navy selection process by performing lots of practice psychometric tests. I noticed that I was getting a number of basic questions wrong, so in order to improve I decided to get some personal tuition at my college to ensure that I could pass this part of the test. Finally, I would say that one of my biggest strengths is that I'm a great team player. I really enjoy working in a team environment and achieving things through a collaborative approach. For example, I play in a local rugby team and we recently won the league trophy for the first time since the club was established some 50 years ago.

Sample interview question 13

What are your weaknesses?

This is a difficult question to answer. We all have weaknesses and anyone who says they haven't, is probably not telling the truth. However, you must be very careful how you respond to this question. Apart from being truthful you must also provide a weakness that you are working hard to improve. You should also remember that you are joining a disciplined service that requires hard work, determination and a will to succeed. So, if you are the type of person who cannot get up in the morning and you keep making regular mistakes at work or at school, then the Royal Navy might not be for you.

The key to responding to this type of question is to be truthful but to also back it up with examples of what you are doing to improve your weakness. Look at the following example.

Sample response to interview question 13

What are your weaknesses?

I have to be honest; while studying for the Royal Navy Recruiting Test I found that I wasn't particularly good at the

sample numerical reasoning questions. Even though I did all right in my Maths GCSE at school, I seemed to be struggling with these questions. Anyway, I didn't let this deter me in my pursuit of joining the Navy so I decided to get some personal tuition at my local college. I managed to find a free evening class that helped me to understand how to carry out the questions. After a couple of weeks' tuition I soon noticed a big improvement in my scores and my ability to answer these questions. I'm still attending the evening classes which I've found to be a great boost to my confidence. I feel very confident that when I do come to sit the tests I'll be able to achieve the required scores.

Sample interview question 14

Can you tell me what you have learnt about your chosen career?

Once again, this is an almost guaranteed question, so make sure you prepare for it fully. The only information you will need is either provided in the recruitment literature, or on the Royal Navy website at www.royalnavy.mod.uk. For example, if you want to join the Royal Navy as a Warfare Specialist then I advise that you read up on the information available regarding this career. Below is a sample response to this question for somebody who is hoping to join as Aircraft Engineering Technician. Use the example to create your own response relevant to your chosen career.

You may even wish to look at other avenues of research to improve your knowledge and further demonstrate your determination to succeed. For example, if you hope to join as a Chef then why not buy a book relating to this field or embark on an evening class and start learning before you even join?

Sample response to interview question 14

Can you tell me what you have learnt about your chosen career?

Chosen career – Aircraft Engineering Technician

I understand that an Aircraft Engineering Technician is a multi-skilled member of the team. Part of the role is to check and repair the Royal Navy's aircraft to ensure that they remain at the peak of readiness. This helps to keep the Service as powerful in the air as it is by land and sea. The Royal Navy operates both fast jets and helicopters from onshore airbases and ocean-going aircraft carriers. Other vessels, such as frigates, also have a single helicopter onboard. In a training or search and rescue squadron, the aircraft operate from land and this is the place that I would carry out my professional training. I understand that Royal Navy aircraft are highly technical and finely tuned machines. They are fitted with state-of-the-art systems for navigation, detection and attack – equipped to fly in adverse conditions and kitted out for the multiple jobs they do. Therefore, they need skilled technicians to look after them and keep them operational.

Sample interview question 15

What has attracted you to your chosen career?

This type of question is designed to see if there are any genuine reasons why you have chosen your particular career. Some applicants get carried away with the glamour of some of the posts that are available, without putting any serious thought into why they actually want the job. When preparing your response to this question you need to think about the skills you have already gained that are relevant to the role, and also any experiences you have that would assist you in becoming competent at that role. For example, an applicant who has been working as a chef in a local restaurant or pub would have plenty of skills and experiences that are relevant to the role.

Previous experiences and skills are not prerequisites for some jobs in the Royal Navy; however, you will need to provide genuine reasons why you have chosen your particular career. The following sample response to this question will assist you during your preparation.

Sample response to interview question 15

What has attracted you to your chosen career?

(Response for applicant applying to become a Steward)

I have always had a passion for working in the hospitality industry. Ever since I was young I have had a keen interest in this area and my grades at college will reflect that. After school had finished I embarked on a Professional Hospitality Diploma which I loved and passed with excellent grades. More recently I have been working part time as a waiter at a local hotel. It made sense to me to chose a job in the Royal Navy that is both relevant to my skills and experiences, and also a job that I will never become bored with. I often receive positive feedback from the customers who come to the hotel, and that makes the hard work and training worthwhile. Because of my experiences as a waiter, and the training and qualifications I have already gained, I believe I would be a great asset to the team.

Sample interview question 16

What are the different ranks for both Royal Navy officers and ratings?

This question assesses your knowledge of the ranks within the Royal Navy. It is a simple question and one that should be relatively easy to respond to. Having an understanding of the different ranks for both commissioned and non-commissioned staff will be an obvious advantage when you start your initial training. Below are the ranks within the Royal Navy:

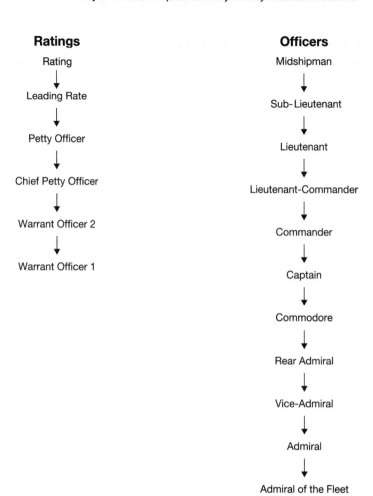

Ratings	Officers
Rating	Midshipman
Leading Rate	Sub-Lieutenant
Petty Officer	Lieutenant
Chief Petty Officer	Lieutenant-Commander
Warrant Officer 2	Commander
Warrant Officer 1	Captain
	Commodore
	Rear Admiral
	Vice-Admiral
	Admiral
	Admiral of the Fleet

You may also decide to study the different badges for each rank prior to your interview. These can be viewed at the Royal Navy's website www.royalnavy.mod.uk.

Sample interview question 17

Tell me about your basic training. What will you go through?

If you have an idea of the type of training that you'll undergo when you join the Royal Navy there is a greater chance that you'll successfully pass it. Conversely, if you have no idea of the type and duration of training that you will go through then it is more likely to come as a shock. I would also advise that, in addition to learning the Phase One training schedule, you learn about the training you will undergo for your chosen career.

Look at the following response to this question, which relates to your Phase One training.

Sample response to interview question 17

Tell me about your basic training. What will you go through?

(Correct at the time of writing)

Basic training takes place at HMS Raleigh in Torpoint. It's a nine-week course which starts on a Sunday evening. During the first week of the course there will be administration and an initial 28-day contract that I will be required to sign. I will also undergo medical and dental checks before starting team exercises where I will interact with the other recruits. In addition to a boat trip and lessons about the sea, I will need to take the Pre-Joining Fitness Test and also a swimming test.

During the second week we'll be introduced to drill and we will get the chance to take part in a parade towards the end of the week. We will also commence the Naval General Training syllabus which will teach us all about Health and Safety, Security and Naval Law.

Week three is very intensive and consists of more squad and marching drills. We will visit a decommissioned submarine

and a ship in Devonport where we will also get the chance to speak to serving sailors about life in the service. Towards the end of the week we will go to Pier Cellars where we will undertake a variety of outdoor activities and team-building exercises.

Week four concentrates on military training and the use of weapons such as the SA80 and the Casco baton. We will learn how to handle the weapons safely and we will be assessed on our firing capabilities. At the weekend of week four we will take part in sporting activities and we will also get ready for the major kit inspection which will take place in week five.

At the start of week five we will undertake the kit inspection, and if we pass we will receive extra privileges. We will also be required to undertake a fitness test. During week five we will camp out on Dartmoor and learn how to use a map and compass.

Week six involves comprehensive seamanship skills including bends and hitches, sea survival, sea replenishment and berthing. We'll also get to spend some time on HMS Brecon where we will be tested against our new skills.

During week seven we will need to undertake another major kit inspection and a fitness test which involves a timed 2.4-km run. We will partake in an obstacle course as part of a team competing against other recruits on the course.

Week eight involves further intensive training, this time in the area of CBRNDC which stands for Chemical, Biological, Radiation, Nuclear and Damage Control. We will also receive training and an assessment in First Aid before sitting the Naval General Training exam and further assault course assessments.

Week nine is passing out week, providing we have passed all of our exams and assessments. The week starts off with a 'Best Mess Competition'. This is basically a competition

to see which mess is the cleanest and best presented. After the competition we will undertake the Final Military Exercise which is scheduled for Wednesday of that week. The last two days of the week are reserved for preparing for pass out.

Now that we have looked at a number of sample interview questions we will round off this section with some important interview tips.

CHAPTER 13
INTERVIEW TIPS

In this chapter are some tips that will help you prepare for the Royal Navy selection interviews. Remember that your success will depend very much on how prepared you are. Don't forget to work on your interview technique, carry out plenty of research and work on your responses to the interview questions.

- In the build-up to the interview carry out plenty of targeted preparation work. Read your recruitment literature and spend time studying the Royal navy website. Ask the Armed Forces Careers office recruitment adviser to provide you with further information about the training you'll undergo for both your chosen career and also your initial training.

- Work on your interview technique and make sure you try out at least one mock interview. This involves getting your family or friends to sit you down and ask you the interview questions that are contained within this book.

- When you receive your date for the interview make sure you turn up on time. Check your travel and parking

arrangements the day before your interview. The last thing you need is to be late for your interview!

- Think carefully about what you are going to wear during the interview. I am not saying that you should go out and buy an expensive suit but I do recommend you make an effort to dress smartly. Having said that, if you do decide to wear a smart suit or formal outfit make sure it is clean and pressed. You can still look scruffy in a suit.

- Personal hygiene is all part and parcel of Royal Navy life. Don't attend the interview unwashed, dirty or fresh from the building site!

- When you walk into the interview room, stand up straight with your shoulders back. Project an image of confidence and be polite, courteous and respectful to the interviewer at all times.

- Don't sit down in the interview chair until invited to do so. This will display good manners.

- While you are in the interview chair sit upright with your hands resting on your knees, palms facing downwards. It is acceptable to use your hands expressively, but don't overdo it.

- Don't slouch in the chair. At the end of each question readjust your position.

- While responding to the interview questions make sure you speak up and be positive. You will need to demonstrate a level of motivation and enthusiasm during the interview.

- Go the extra mile and learn a little bit about the Royal Navy's history. When the members of the panel ask you 'What can you tell us about the Royal Navy?' you will be able to demonstrate that you have made an effort to look into its history as well as its modern-day activities.

- Ask positive questions at the end of the interview. Don't ask questions such as 'How much leave will I get?' or 'How often do I get paid?'

- If you are unsure about a question don't 'waffle'. If you do not know the answer, then it is all right to say so. Move on to the next question and put it behind you.

- Finally, believe in yourself and be confident.

ROYAL NAVY QUIZ

This Royal Navy quiz will help you during your preparation for the interview. The second part of the quiz features a number of history questions. It is not essential to learn everything about the history of the Royal Navy for selection purposes but by learning key dates, ships, battles and people you will be demonstrating a keen interest in the amazing history of this special service.

In order to answer the questions in the quiz you will need to carry out your own independent research. You will be able to find the information you need in order to answer the questions both in this book and also on the Royal Navy website; www. royalnavy.mod.uk.

Quiz 1 – General Royal Navy questions

Question I

How many weeks is the initial Royal Navy basic training course for a Rating?

Answer

Question 2

For how long is the initial contract that you sign during the first week of basic training?

Answer

Question 3

During which week of basic training is the first Divisional kit inspection?

Answer

Question 4

What is the highest rank for ratings?

Answer

Question 5

Where is the Navy Command Headquarters based?

Answer

Question 6

Who has full command of the Royal Navy Fleet and is responsible for the Fleet element of military operational capability?

Answer

Question 7

What is the name of the flag that is flown by all HM ships in commission and by shore establishments?

Answer

Question 8

What is the name given to the procedure where a Royal Navy ship is re-supplied with fuel, food, stores and ammunition while at sea?

Answer

Question 9

hat is the highest officer rank in the Royal Navy?

Answer

Question 10

At cruising speed, what is the maximum distance a Royal Navy frigate can travel?

Answer

Question 11

At cruising speed, what is the maximum distance a Royal Navy destroyer can travel?

Answer

Question 12

Which of the following is not a Type 23 Duke Class frigate?

HMS *Argyll*   HMS *Lancaster*   HMS *Gloucester*
HMS *Iron Duke*

Answer

Question 13

Which of the following is not a Type 42 destroyer?

HMS *Liverpool*   HMS *Edinburgh*   HMS *York*
HMS *Daring*

Answer

Question 14

Which of the following is not a Naval Air Squadron?

NAS 800   NAS 727   NAS 820   NAS 814
NAS 722

Answer

Question 15

In 2002, which of the following Royal Navy training establishments became the lead establishment for the Maritime Warfare School (MWS)?

HMS *Excellent*   HMS *Collingwood*   HMS *Sultan*
HMS *Dartmouth*

Answer

Question 16

Which of the following Royal Navy training establishments is home of the Royal Naval School of Marine Engineering (RNSME) and the Royal Naval Air Engineering and Survival School (RNAESS)?

HMS *Excellent*   HMS *Collingwood*   HMS *Sultan*
HMS *Dartmouth*

Answer

Question 17

What is the mission statement of the Royal Naval Chaplaincy Service?

Answer

Question 18

What standard of swimming should you reach before joining the Royal Navy?

Answer

Question 19

What is the name of the cup which is presented to a recruit who has achieved outstanding results throughout their initial Phase One Training having overcome personal adverse difficulties?

Answer

Question 20

What is the name of the cup which is awarded at the end of Phase One training to the class which shows the best skill at Weapon Drill and Marching?

Answer

Answers to Quiz 1

1. Nine weeks

2. 28 days

3. Week 5

4. Warrant Officer 1

5. Portsmouth

6. Commander in Chief Fleet

7. White Ensign

8. Replenishment at Sea or RAS

9. Admiral of the Fleet

10. 7500 miles

11. 4000 miles

12. HMS *Gloucester*

13. HMS *Daring*

14. NAS 722

15. HMS *Collingwood*

16. HMS *Dartmouth*

17. 'Naval Chaplains; friends and advisors to all onboard'

18. Be capable of swimming at least 50 metres unaided and be able to tread water for 1 minure without additional clothing.

19. The Stuart Cup

20. The Howe Trophy

Quiz 2 – Royal Navy History

Question I

In which year did the Falklands conflict commence?

Answer

Question 2

In which year was the Royal Navy surface fleet reorganised into two flotillas?

Answer

Question 3

At the current time how many nuclear submarines are there?

Answer

Question 4

In which year did the Battle of Jutland commence?

Answer

Question 5

Which ship was Admiral Jellicoe's flagship during the Battle of Jutland?

Answer

Question 6

In which year was the Battle of Trafalgar?

Answer

Question 7

Between 1807 and 1866, the Royal Navy captured how many slave ships?

Answer

Question 8

In which year did Admiral Fisher become First Sea Lord?

Answer

Question 9

Which two aircraft carriers were involved in the Falklands conflict?

Answer

Question 10

Who was the naval commander for Operation 'Overlord' during the invasion of Normandy in 1944?

Answer

Question II

What was the name of Britain's first nuclear powered submarine?

Answer

Question I2

Which battle occurred during November 1759?

Answer

Question I3

Which ship was originally laid down in 1915 as a large light cruiser which mounted two 457 mm guns?

Answer

Question I4

Which ship is probably the most famous ship in the history of the Royal Navy and is best known as Nelson's flagship during the Battle of Trafalgar?

Answer

Question I5

During which year was the Battle of Cape Matapan?

Answer

Question 16

Which battle took place in the Canary Islands during April 1657?

Answer

Question 17

How did the 'Mary Rose' get its name?

Answer

Question 18

In which year was James Cook promoted to Captain?

Answer

Question 19

Which ship captured USS *Chesapeake* off Boston in June 1813?

Answer

Question 20

Who was in overall command of the Falklands conflict?

Answer

Answers to Quiz 2

1. 1982

2. 2002

3. 16

4. 1916

5. HMS *Iron Duke*

6. 1805

7. More than 500

8. 1904

9. HMS *Invincible* and HMS *Hermes*

10. Admiral Bertram Ramsay

11. HMS *Dreadnought*

12. The Battle of Quiberon Bay

13. HMS *Furious*

14. HMS *Victory*

15. 1941

16. The Battle of Santa Cruz

17. It was named after King Henry VIII's sister Mary and the Tudor emblem, the rose.

18. 1775

19. HMS *Shannon*

20. Commander in Chief Fleet, Admiral Sir John Fieldhouse

FREE BONUS GUIDE – HOW TO GET NAVY FIT

Introduction

Welcome to your 'How to Get Navy Fit' information guide. Within this guide I have provided a number of exercises and tips that will assist you during your preparation for your initial basic training course and also for the Pre-Joining Fitness Test (PJFT). The PJFT is usually carried out at a gymnasium or fitness centre.

Your preparation for passing the Royal Navy selection process should include a structured fitness training programme. Do not make the mistake of solely working on your interview skills or your academic ability. If I was going through selection now I would vary my academic studies and my knowledge of the Navy study with a proper structured fitness training programme. For example, if I had scheduled in 60 minutes' psychometric test preparation on a particular weekday evening, then I would most probably go for a three-mile run immediately afterwards. This would allow me to free my mind

from the high concentration levels of studying. In addition to improving your physical fitness levels, you should keep an eye on your diet and eat healthy foods while drinking plenty of water. This will all go a long way to helping you improve your general well-being and concentration levels.

As with any form of exercise you should consult your doctor first.

WARNING – Ensure you take advice from a competent fitness trainer in relation to the correct execution of any of the exercises contained within this guide. You may find that the techniques described in this guide differ from the requirements of the Royal Navy.

Preparing for the PJFT, Recruit Course and Navy life

Let's look at some of the types of activities you'll be expected to undertake during training and your career.

Common activities

Running   Obviously during your initial Royal Navy basic training course you will be doing plenty of running. You will be required to take further fitness tests in addition to the initial PJFT. The most effective way to prepare for the large amount of running is to integrate a running programme into your action plan.

Lifting   During your Royal Navy basic training, and also during the entirety of your career you'll be required to lift heavy objects. During my time in the Fleet Air Arm I worked with weapons and ejector seats. This kind of work involved heavy lifting at times, especially when lifting sidewinder missiles onto Sea Harriers. The most effective types of exercise to carry out in order to develop your lower and upper body strength include press-ups, sit-ups, squats and swimming. You should also practise correct manual handling techniques; details can be found later in this section.

Pulling   Once again, during your career and basic training you will be required to pull heavy objects, especially onboard ship. The most effective types of exercise that will develop the muscles for lifting include squats, lunges, indoor rowing and pull-ups.

Before we move on to each of the core exercises required to develop your stamina and fitness levels for the above areas, let's look at some important planning tips.

Planning your workouts and preparing for the Pre-Joining Fitness Test

The key to a successful fitness preparation strategy is variety and continual improvement. When you commence your fitness programme you should be highly motivated. The hard part will come a couple of weeks into your fitness programme when your rate of improvement decreases. It is at this point that you must vary your exercise routine in order to ensure that you stay on the right track and don't lose interest. The reason why most people give up their fitness regime is mainly due to a lack of proper preparation. You will recall that throughout this book the word 'preparation' has been integral, and the same word applies when preparing for the PJFT. Preparation is key to your success and it is essential that you plan your workouts effectively.

Members of the Armed Forces are required to maintain high fitness levels. However, some branches of the Armed Forces require a higher standard than others and your fitness training programme should reflect this. For example, a candidate who is applying to join the Royal Marines or the Parachute Regiment would concentrate a lot more effort on their fitness preparation than, say, somebody who was applying to join the Royal Navy as a Rating. Work hard to pass the PJFT but do not spend hours and hours at the gym or out running.

Read on for some great ways not only to pass the Pre-Joining Fitness Test, but also to stay Navy fit all year round.

Get an assessment before you start training

The first step is to conduct a 'self-fitness test'. This should involve the following three areas:

1. A 1.5-mile run in the fastest time possible.

2. As many sit-ups as possible in two minutes.

3. As many press-ups as possible in two minutes.

The tests will be easy to perform and you will not need to attend a gym in order to carry them out. However, the 1.5-mile run that forms part of the PJFT is usually carried out on a treadmill. Running on a treadmill requires a different technique from running on the road. While not essential, I would recommend you try running on a treadmill prior to the actual PJFT so that you can become familiar with the technique required.

Once you have done all three tests you should write down your results and keep them safe somewhere. After two weeks of following your new fitness regime, do all three tests again and check your results against the previous results. This is a great way to monitor your performance and progress and it will also keep you motivated and focused on your goals. In addition to the above three tests, I would recommend that you include swimming practice in your fitness routine. During your initial Royal Navy basic training course you will be required to pass a swimming test which includes treading water while clothed. If you cannot swim now is a good time to get some lessons at your local pool.

Keep a check on what you eat and drink

Before we get started with stretching and targeted exercises to prepare you for life in the Royal Navy, I would recommend that you write down everything you eat and drink for a whole week. You must include tea, water, milk, biscuits and anything – everything that you digest. You will

soon begin to realise how much you are eating and you will notice areas in which you can make some changes. For example, if you are taking sugar with your tea then why not try reducing it or giving it up all together? If you do then you will soon notice the difference. Because you are about to embark on a fitness training routine you will need to fill your body with the right type of fuel. This includes both food and drink. Let's get one thing straight from the offset: if you fill your body with rubbish then your fitness performance is likely to be on a par with rubbish. Fill it with the right nutrients and vitamins then you will perform far more effectively. When I was 26 years old I decided to do my own version of the iron man challenge for a local charity. I swam two miles, then I ran a marathon, before finally completing a 120-mile cycle ride, all one after the other! I managed to raise more than £10,000 for a children's hospice in Kent. In the six months prior to the challenge I trained very hard, but I also put just as much effort into what I ate and drank. This proved crucial to my success in achieving the challenge.

During your fitness training programme I would recommend you totally avoid the high calorie foods that lack the right level of nutrients such as chips, burgers, chocolates, sweets, fizzy drinks and alcohol. Instead, replace them with fruit, vegetables, pasta, rice, chicken and fish. You also need to make sure you drink plenty of water throughout the day in order to keep yourself fully hydrated. This will help to keep up your concentration levels for the Royal Navy Recruiting Test. Many people who keep fit use vitamin supplements and energy enhancing drinks. It is my opinion that you don't need any of these providing you drink plenty of water and you stick to a balanced diet that includes the right vitamins and nutrients. Spend your hard-earned money on something else instead of buying supplements, powders and energy drinks. It is important that you start to look for opportunities to improve your fitness and well-being right from the offset. These areas are what I call 'easy wins'.

You don't need to lift heavy weights in order to pass the PJFT

When I applied to join the Fire Service the physical tests were rigorous, demanding and extremely difficult to pass. As part of the assessment I was required to bench press 50 kg, 20 times within 60 seconds. It is my strong belief that you do not need to lift heavy weights in order to pass the Royal Navy PJFT. In fact, I would go as far as to say that you don't need to lift any weights at all, other than your own body weight during press-ups. If you do decide to lift weights then you will be better off including some form of light weight work which is specifically targeted at increasing stamina, strength and endurance. Instead of performing bench presses in the gym, replace them with press-ups. Instead of performing heavy lateral pull-down exercises, replace them with pull-ups which utilise only your own body weight.

There are some great exercises contained in this guide and most of them can be carried out without the need to attend a gym.

One step at a time

Only you will know how fit you are. I advise that you first write down the areas that you believe or feel you need to improve on. For example, if after carrying out your three self-fitness tests you realise that you are going to struggle to pass the PJFT then embark on a structured running programme that is designed to gradually improve your performance.

The key to making improvements is to do it gradually, one step at a time. Try to set yourself small goals. When you carry out your initial self-fitness test you may find that you can achieve only a few press-ups and sit-ups. Instead of focusing on a higher target of 50-press ups within two minutes, break down your goals into easy-to-achieve stepping stones. For example, by the end of the first week aim to do an additional 10 press-ups and sit-ups. Then, add another 10 to the second weeks' target, and so on. One of the biggest problems that

many people encounter when starting a fitness regime is they become bored very quickly. This leads to a lack of motivation and desire, and soon the fitness programme stops. Change your exercise routine often in order to maintain your interest levels. Instead of running every day, try swimming, indoor rowing or cycling. This will keep your interest and motivational levels high and it will also work other muscle groups that running cannot touch.

Stretching

How many people stretch before carrying out any form of exercise? Very few people is the correct answer. Not only is it irresponsible but it is also placing yourself at high risk from injury. The last thing you need is an injury prior to PJFT, especially after the amount of hard work you will be putting in to ensure you pass. Before I commence with the exercises we will take a look at a few warm-up stretches. Make sure you stretch fully before carrying out any exercises. You want your Royal Navy career to be a long one and that means looking after yourself, including stretching! It is also very important to check with your GP that you are medically fit to carry out any form of physical exercise.

The warm-up calf stretch

To perform this stretch effectively you should start by facing a wall while standing upright. Your right foot should be close to the wall and your right knee bent. Now place your hands flat against the wall and at a height that is level with your shoulders. Stretch your left leg far out behind you without lifting your toes and heel off the floor, and lean towards the wall (see diagram over page).

Once you have performed this stretch for 25 seconds switch, legs and carry out the same procedure for the right leg. As with all exercises contained within this guide, stop if you feel any pain or discomfort.

Stretching the shoulder muscles

Stand with your feet slightly apart and with your knees only slightly bent. Now hold your arms straight out in front of you and with your palms facing away from you and your fingers pointing skywards. Now place your right palm on the back of your left hand and use it to push the left hand further away from you. If you are performing this exercise correctly you will feel the muscles in your shoulder stretching. Hold for 10 seconds before switching sides.

Stretching the quad muscles (front of the thigh)

Before you carry out any form of running it is imperative that you stretch your leg muscles. As you are already aware, as part of the PJFT you are required to run a set distance in a set period of time. It is very important that you stretch fully before the test and your instructor should take you through a number of stretching exercises before you jump on the treadmill.

To begin with, stand with your left hand pressed against a wall or firm surface. Bend your left knee slightly and bring your right heel up to your bottom while grasping your foot with your right hand (see diagram above). Your back should be straight and your shoulders, hips and knees should all be

in line at all times during the exercise. Hold for 25 seconds before switching legs.

Stretching the hamstring muscles (back of the thigh)

It is very easy to injure your hamstring muscles as a Royal Navy Rating, especially with all of the running you'll be doing during your initial basic training. Therefore, you must get into the routine of stretching out the hamstring muscles before every training session.

To perform this exercise correctly, stand up straight and place your right foot on a table or other firm surface so that your leg is almost parallel to the floor. Keep your left leg straight and your foot at a right angle to your leg. Start to move your hands slowly down your right leg towards your ankle until you feel tension on the underside of your thigh. When you feel this tension you know that you are starting to stretch the hamstring muscles. Hold for 25 seconds before switching legs.

I have covered only a small number of stretching exercises here; however, it is crucial that you stretch fully in all areas before carrying out any of the following exercises. Remember to obtain professional advice before carrying out any type of exercise.

Running

One of the great ways to prepare for the Pre-Joining Fitness Test is to embark on a structured running programme. You do not need to run extremely long distances in order to gain massively from this type of exercise. As part of the PJFT you will be required to run 1.5 miles in a set period of time. Don't settle for the minimum standard but instead keep pushing yourself and improving your stamina/fitness levels.

Towards the end of this guide are a number of weekly training programmes for you to follow. These incorporate running and

series of combined exercises that will help you to prepare for the PJFT and the swimming test.

Tips for running

- As with any exercise you should consult a doctor before taking part to make sure that you are medically fit.

- It is certainly worth investing in a pair of comfortable running shoes that serve the purpose for your intended training programme. Your local sports shop will be able to advise you on the types that are best for you. You don't have to spend a fortune to buy a good pair of running shoes.

- It is a good idea to invest in a 'high visibility' jacket or coat so that you can be seen by fast-moving traffic if you intend to run on or near the road.

- Make sure you carry out at least five minutes of stretching exercises not only before but also after your running programme. This can help to prevent injury.

- While you shouldn't run on a full stomach, it is not good to run on an empty one either. A great food to eat approximately 30 minutes before a run is a banana. This will give you energy.

- Drink plenty of water throughout the day. Drink at least 1.5 litres each day in total. This will keep you hydrated and help to prevent muscle cramp.

- Don't overdo it. If you feel any pain or discomfort then stop and seek medical advice.

- When preparing for the Royal Navy selection process, use your exercise time as a break from your studies. For example, if you have been practising for the Recruiting Test for an hour why not take a break and go running? When you return from your run you can concentrate on your studies feeling refreshed.

Exercises to improve your overall stamina and fitness levels

Press-ups

While running is a great way to improve your overall fitness, you will also need to carry out exercises that are designed to improve your upper body strength. These exercises will help you to prepare for the Royal Navy basic training course.

The great thing about press-ups is that you don't have to attend a gym to perform them. However, you must ensure that you can perform them correctly as injury can occur. You need to spend only five minutes every day on press-ups, possibly after you go running or even before if you prefer. If you are not used to doing press-ups then start slowly and aim to carry out at least 10.

Even if you struggle to do just 10, you will soon find that after a few days' practice you will be up to 20 or more.

Step 1 – Lie on a mat or even surface. Your hands should be shoulder width apart and your arms fully extended.

Step 2 – Gradually lower your body until the elbows reach 90°. Do not rush the movement as you may cause injury.

Step 3 – Once your elbows reach 90° slowly return to the starting position with your arms fully extended.

The press-up action should be a continuous movement with no rest. However, it is important that the exercise is as smooth as possible and there should be no jolting or sudden movements. Complete as many press-ups as possible and always keep a record of how many you do. This will keep your focus and also maintain your motivation levels.

Sit-ups

Sit-ups are great for building the core stomach muscles. Strong abdominal muscles are important for lifting items of equipment, something which is integral to the role of a Royal Navy Rating.

Lie flat on your back with your knees bent at a 45° angle and with your feet together. Your hands can either be crossed on your chest, by your sides, or cupped behind your ears as indicated in the diagram over page.

Without moving your lower body, curl your upper torso upwards and in towards your knees, until your shoulder blades are as high off the ground as possible. As you reach the highest point, tighten your abdominal muscles for a few seconds. This will allow you to get the most out of the exercise. Now slowly start to lower yourself back to the starting position. You should aim to work up to at least 50 effective sit-ups within a two-minute period. You will be amazed at how quickly this can be achieved and you will begin to notice your stomach muscles developing.

 how2become

Squats (these work the legs and bottom)

Squats are a great exercise for working the leg muscles. They are the perfect exercise in your preparation for PJFT as they will develop the leg muscles used for running.

Stand up straight with your arms at your sides. Concentrate on keeping your feet shoulder-width apart and your head up. Do not look downwards at any point during the exercise. You will see from the diagram opposite that the person has their lower back slightly arched. They are also holding light weights which can add to the intensity of the exercise.

Now start to bend your knees very slowly while pushing your rear out as though you are about to sit down on a chair. Keep lowering yourself down until your thighs reach past the 90° point. Make sure your weight is on your heels so that your knees do not extend over your toes. At this point you may wish to tighten your thighs and buttocks to intensify the exercise.

As you come back up to a standing position, push down through your heels which will allow you to maintain your balance. Repeat the exercise 15 to 20 times.

Lunges (these work the thighs and bottom)

You will have noticed throughout this guide that these simple, yet highly effective exercises can be carried out at home. The lunge exercise is another great addition to the range of exercises that require no attendance at the gym, and they also fit perfectly into the role of a Royal Navy Rating, simply because they concentrate on building the necessary core muscles to perform the demanding tasks of the job such as bending down and picking up items of equipment.

Stand with your back straight and your feet together (you may hold light hand weights if you wish to add some intensity to the exercise).

Take a big step forwards as illustrated in the diagram above making sure you inhale as you go and landing with the heel first. Bend the front knee no more than 90° so as to avoid injury. Keep your back straight and lower the back knee as close to the floor as possible. Your front knee should be lined up over your ankle and your back thigh should be in line with your back.

To complete the exercise, exhale and push down against your front heel, squeezing your buttocks tight as you rise back to the starting position.

Repeat the exercise 15 to 20 times before switching sides.

Tricep dips

Tricep dips are brilliant at building the muscles at the rear of the arm. Because the tricep muscle is a core part of upper

body strength you should spend time developing it. Once again, you do not have to attend a gym to work on it.

Step 1 – Place your hands shoulder-width apart on a bench or immovable object as per the diagram.

Step 2 – Lower your body until your elbows are at an angle of 90°.

Step 3 – Push back up so the body returns to the starting position, breathing out on the way up. Ensure that your back remains close to the bench or immovable object throughout the movement.

This exercise will allow you to improve on your upper and lower body strength, which will in turn improve your ability to pass the PJFT and the initial basic training course.

Pull-ups

Pull-ups are another great way for building the core upper body muscle groups which Royal Navy ratings use while climbing ladders onboard ship and lifting heavy items of equipment. The unfortunate thing about this type of exercise

is you will probably need to attend a gym in order to carry it out. Having said that, there are a number of different types of 'pull-up bars' available to buy on the market that can easily and safely be fitted to a doorway at home. If you choose to purchase one of these items make sure that it conforms to the relevant safety standards first.

Lateral pull-ups are very effective at increasing upper body strength. If you have access to a gymnasium then these can be practised on a 'lateral pull-down' machine. It is advised that you consult a qualified gym instructor before you attempt this exercise.

Pull-ups should be performed by grasping firmly a sturdy and solid bar. Before you grasp the bar make sure it is safe. Your

hands should be roughly shoulder-width apart. Straighten your arms so that your body hangs loose. You will feel your lateral muscles and biceps stretching as you hang in the air. This is the starting position for the lateral pull-up exercise.

Next, pull yourself upwards to the point where your chest is almost touching the bar and your chin is actually over the bar. While pulling upwards, focus on keeping your body straight without any arching or swinging as this can result in injury. Once your chin is over the bar, you can lower yourself back down to the initial starting position. Repeat the exercise 10 times.

Alternative exercises

Swimming

Apart from press-ups, lateral raises and the other exercises in this guide, another fantastic way to improve your upper body and overall fitness is to swim. You will also need to be able to pass a swimming test once you start your basic training course. If you have access to a swimming pool, and you can swim, then this is a brilliant way to improve your fitness and especially your upper body strength. If you are not a great swimmer you can start off with short distances and gradually build up your swimming strength and stamina. You may also decide to get some swimming lessons at your local pool. Breaststroke is sufficient for building good upper body strength providing you put the effort into swimming an effective number of lengths. You may wish to alternate your running programme with the odd day of swimming. If you can swim 10 lengths of a 25-metre pool initially this is a good base to start from. You will soon find that you can increase this number easily providing that you carry on swimming every week. Try running to your local swimming pool if it is not too far away, swimming 20 lengths of breaststroke, and then running back home.

This is a great way to combine your fitness activity and prevent yourself from becoming bored with your training programme.

 how2become

The multi-stage fitness test or bleep test

A great way to build endurance and stamina is by training with the multi-stage fitness test or bleep test as it is otherwise called. The multi-stage fitness test is used by sports coaches and trainers to estimate an athlete's VO_2 max (maximum oxygen uptake). The test is especially useful for players of sports like football, hockey or rugby. The test itself can be obtained through various websites on the internet and it is great for building your endurance and stamina levels.

Training programmes

I believe it is important to add some form of structure to your training programme. Apart from keeping you focused and motivated it will also allow you to measure your results. If I was going through selection now I would get myself a small notebook and pencil and keep a check of my times, distances, repetitions and exercises. I would try to improve in each area as each week passes. In order to help you add some form of structure to your training regime I have provided four sample training programmes of differing intensity. Before you carry out any form of exercise make sure you consult your doctor to ensure you are fit and healthy. Start off slowly and gradually increase the pace and intensity of your exercises.

You will notice that each of the exercises is specifically designed to increase your ability during the PJFT and the basic training course.

Training programme 1

Day 1	Day 2	Day 3	Day 4	Day 5
1.5-mile run (best effort). Record and keep results	3-mile run	Swimming (500 metres) or indoor rowing for 2000 metres	3-mile run	Swimming (500 metres) or indoor rowing for 2000 metres
50 sit-ups and 50 press-ups or as many as possible	50 sit-ups and 50 press-ups or as many as possible	10-mile cycle ride	50 sit-ups and 50 press-ups or as many as possible	50 sit-ups and 50 press-ups or as many as possible
3-mile walk at a brisk pace		20 lunges each side and 30 star jumps		3-mile walk at a brisk pace

Days 6 and 7 = Rest days

Training programme 2

Day 1	Day 2	Day 3	Day 4	Day 5
1.5-mile run (best effort). Record and keep results	Swimming (500 metres) or indoor rowing for 3000 metres	5-mile run	2-mile walk at a brisk pace followed by a 3-mile run	Swimming (1000 metres) or indoor rowing for 3000 metres
50 sit-ups and 50 press-ups or as many as possible	10-mile cycle ride	50 sit-ups and 50 press-ups or as many as possible		50 sit-ups and 50 press-ups or as many as possible
30 squat thrusts	20 lunges each side and 30 star jumps	Pull-ups (as many as possible)	Pull-ups (as many as possible)	30 squat thrusts, 20 lunges each side and 30 star jumps

Days 6 and 7 = Rest days

Training programme 3

Day 1	Day 2	Day 3	Day 4	Day 5
1.5-mile run (best effort). Record and keep results	5-mile run	20-mile cycle ride	5-mile run	Swimming (1000 metres)
50 sit-ups and 50 press-ups or as many as possible	50 sit-ups and 50 press-ups or as many as possible	3-mile walk at a brisk pace	50 sit-ups and 50 press-ups or as many as possible	50 sit-ups and 50 press-ups or as many as possible
Swimming (500 metres)		30 squat thrusts, 20 lunges each side and 30 star jumps		30 squat thrusts, 20 lunges each side and 30 star jumps

Days 6 and 7 = Rest days

Training programme 4

Day 1	Day 2	Day 3	Day 4	Day 5
1.5-mile run (best effort). Record and keep results	Bleep test (best effort)	7-mile run	Swimming (1000 metres)	10-mile run
50 sit-ups and 50 press-ups or as many as possible	Pull-ups (as many as possible) followed by 50 squat thrusts, 25 lunges each side and 50 star jumps	70 sit-ups and 70 press-ups or as many as possible	Pull-ups (as many as possible) followed by 50 squat thrusts, 25 lunges each side and 50 star jumps	70 sit-ups and 70 press-ups or as many as possible
Swimming (1000 metres) followed by a 3-mile brisk walk	20-mile cycle ride	30 squat thrusts, 20 lunges each side and 30 star jumps	10-mile cycle ride	Swimming (500 metres) followed by a 3-mile brisk walk

Days 6 and 7 = Rest days

Tips for staying with your workout

The hardest part of your training programme will be sticking with it. In this final section of your fitness guide are some useful golden rules that will enable you to maintain your motivation levels in the build-up to the Royal Navy Pre-Joining Fitness Test.

Golden rule 1 – Work out often

Aim to train five times each and every week.

Each training session should last from 20 minutes to a maximum of an hour. The quality of training is important so don't go for heavy weights but instead go for a lighter weight with a better technique. On days when you are feeling energetic, take advantage of this opportunity and do more!

This guide features a number of simple-to-perform exercises that are targeted at the core muscle groups required to pass the PJFT and also to prepare you for your initial basic training course. Between your study sessions, try carrying out these exercises at home or get yourself out on the road running or cycling. Use your study downtime effectively and wisely.

Golden rule 2 – Mix up your exercises

Your exercise programme should include some elements of cardiovascular (running, bleep test, brisk walking, swimming and cycling), resistance training (light weights or own body exercises such as press-ups and sit-ups) and, finally, flexibility (stretching). Make sure that you always warm up and warm down.

If you are a member of a gym consider taking up a class such as Pilates. This type of exercise will teach you how to build core training into your exercise, and show you how to hit your abdominals in ways that are not possible with conventional sit-ups. If you are a member of a gym then a fantastic 'all round' exercise that I strongly recommend is indoor rowing. Rowing will hit every major muscle group in your body and it is also perfect for improving your stamina levels and cardiovascular fitness.

Golden rule 3 – Eat a healthy and balanced diet

It is vitally important that you eat the right fuel to give you the energy to train to your full potential. Don't fill your body with rubbish and then expect to train well. Think about what you are eating and drinking, including the quantities, and keep a record of what you are digesting. You will become stronger and fitter more quickly if you eat small amounts of nutritious foods at short intervals.

Golden rule 4 – Get help

Try working with a personal trainer or someone else who is preparing for selection. They will ensure that you work hard and will help you to achieve your goals. The mere fact that they are there at your side will add an element of competition to your training sessions! A consultation with a professional nutritionist will also help you improve your eating habits and establish your individual food needs.

Golden rule 5 – Fitness is for life

Working out and eating correctly are not short-term projects. They are things that should be as natural to us as brushing our teeth. Make fitness a permanent part of your life by following these tips, and you'll lead a better and more fulfilling life!

Good luck and work hard to improve your weak areas.

A FEW FINAL WORDS

You have now reached the end of the book and no doubt you will be ready to start preparing for the Royal Navy selection process. Just before you go off and start on your preparation, consider the following.

The majority of candidates who pass the Royal Navy selection process have a number of common attitudes. These are as follows:

They believe in themselves

Regardless of what anyone tells you, you *can* pass the selection process and you can achieve high scores. Just like any job of this nature, you have to be prepared to work hard in order to be successful. Remember, when I left school I had very few educational qualifications, but it didn't stop me from achieving what I wanted in life. Make sure you have the self-belief to pass the selection process and fill your mind with positive thoughts.

They prepare fully

Those people who achieve in life prepare fully for every eventuality and that is what you must do when you apply to become a Rating with the Royal Navy. Work hard and especially concentrate on improving your weak areas.

They persevere

Perseverance is a fantastic word. Everybody comes across obstacles or setbacks in their life, but it is what you do about those setbacks that is important. If you fail at something, then ask yourself 'why' you have failed. This will allow you to improve for next time and if you keep improving and trying, success will eventually follow. Adopt this same method of thinking when you apply to join the Royal Navy.

They are self-motivated

How much do you want to join the Navy? Do you want it, or do you *really* want it? When you apply to join you should want it more than anything in the world. Your levels of self-motivation will shine through when you walk into the AFCO and when you attend the interview. For the weeks and months leading up to the selection process, be motivated as best you can and always keep your fitness levels up as this will serve to increase your levels of motivation.

Work hard, stay focused and be what you want . . .

Richard McMunn

INDEX

Visit www.how2become.co.uk to find more related products that will help you to pass this selection process. From the website we can provide you with DVDs and guides that will help you to pass the interview, and other stages of the selection process. We also run one-day intensive training courses that are designed to help you successfully pass the application process for any career.

Visit www.how2become.co.uk for more details.